THE ULTIMATE

Air Fryer

BOOK

365 Days Quick, Healthy, and Mouthwatering Air Fryer Recipes for Beginners to Improve Your Health

Caitlin Hayward

Table of Contents

INTRODUCTION

Congratulations, you are the new owners of an air fryer, or perhaps hoping to be one soon. It seems everyone is talking about owning an air fryer, and you simply need to find out for yourself if the hype holds up.

You want to know how they work. Do they fry? What types of foods can you have in the air fryer? Thankfully, this book will tell you all you need to know about your new air fryer. First, you need to know that air fryers are not deep fryers.

Air fryers use hot air, and that's what makes them special. They are simply small but extremely powerful ovens, and as ovens, they utilise air for heat, while deep-frying uses fat to transfer heat. Since air fryers aren't fryers but ovens, the food you cook in there will not come out identical to something that has been through a deep fryer.

The advantage of air fryers is that they are a lot less oil-intensive and messy compared to deep fryers. Moreover, these little ovens can do much more than cook "fried" food. Air fryers can be used to beautifully brown vegetables, create airy cakes and even put a crust on chicken wings.

Air fryers are designed to use dry heat, so when you think of an air fryer you should think of cooking methods that use dry heat (frying, baking, and roasting) instead of wet heat cooking methods (steaming, braising, and boiling).

The convenience an air fryer provides is one of the reasons why it is so popular. You no longer have to use a lot of oil to cook, which makes whatever you are cooking healthier. Furthermore, there isn't as much mess to clean up with an air fryer. For instance, you must wipe the air fryer down or hand-wash the baskets or components (more on that later). This is compared to a deep fryer that requires you to get rid of the oil before thoroughly scrubbing the deep fryer.

There are various recipes you can use with an air fryer; for one, you can cook pre-fried frozen food such as fish sticks, chicken tenders, pizza rolls, and tater tots. Generally, portion-sized frozen foods and those that come in bite-size pieces can become crisp quickly when using an air fryer.

You can also use from-scratch recipes similar to pre-fried frozen foods, such as air-fried chicken, crab cakes, and air-fried mozzarella sticks. For those trying to eat much healthier, you aren't left out, as you can grill or roast vegetables such as summer squash, broccoli, root vegetables, Brussels sprouts, or cauliflower florets. All of these taste great in an air fryer.

Potatoes make for great cooking in an air fryer, as an air fryer will easily outperform a regular oven. You can get a crispy skin on your chicken wings in no time with an air fryer. This makes an air fryer great for last-minute dinner decisions. Watching the big game and want hot dogs on hand? Then you can cook your franks in the air fryer to give it that ballpark flavour. With an air fryer, your choices are limitless. So limitless that you might want to start keeping an eye on your waistline.

Apart from cooking food from scratch, an air fryer is great for reheating food. Think about it: your air fryer is like a turbocharged oven; unlike a microwave, you can be sure your food won't turn into a mushy mess.

There are so many recipes you can try out with the air fryer in this cookbook. You get a wide array of recipes with easy-to-get ingredients, easy-to-make steps and a whole lot more.

Chapter 1 Air Fryer Basic Guide

Chapter 1 Air Fryer Basic Guide

The first you do when you open your air fryer box is to take out all the removable components. Depending on the type of air fryer you get, you will have a perforated tray or grate located at the bottom of your removable basket. Wash and dry these components before use.

Before using your air fryer, place it on a heat-resistant surface, away from any item. Place the grate, tray and removable basket. Some air fryer manufacturers state that you should first run your air fryer on empty for about 10 minutes before you begin cooking with it. This will let it off-gas. During this process, you might perceive a slightly chemical odour reminiscent of a new appliance smell, so open the windows or turn your vents on. This process is only for newly used air fryers and should not be repeated.

How Does an Air Fryer Work?

As stated earlier, your air fryer is a turbocharged convection oven. It enables you to bake, broil or roast. The only thing you cannot do is deep-fry in it. The way it works is similar to an oven. Since heat rises, the top rack in an oven is usually the hottest spot, leading to uneven cooking. This is why numerous cookie recipes say you should rotate your baking sheets back to front and top to bottom halfway through the baking process.

However, in a convection oven, fans blow that hot air around, so the temperate is equal regardless of where you put your food in the oven. Air fryers take that philosophy to cook your food. The airflow has been designed to closely replicate the heat distribution of a deep fryer.

Five Features of Air Fryers

There are major reasons why air fryers are gaining popularity. Here are the 5 features.

Less fat

With an air fryer, you cook with a lot less oil than you would other conventional methods. Compared to a deep fryer that requires lots of oil for you to cook your food in, an air fryer needs less than a quarter of that. All you have to do is simply lightly brush your food item, and you are set to go. Additionally, you get the health benefit of avoiding the carcinogens that deep-fried foods are typically linked with.

Faster meals

As stated earlier, an air fryer gives you the ability to make meals quicker. Due to the way the air fryer works, hot air circulates around your food to ensure that your food is cooked more quickly. Compared to toaster ovens or conventional ovens, an air fryer preheats and cooks your food in just a fraction of the time.

Most air fryers can preheat to 400 F in less than 5 minutes, compared to gas ovens, which take up to 15 minutes to get to the same temperature. Electric ovens can take 20 minutes to get to the same temperature. This short preheat time significantly

reduces the time it takes to cook your food.

Air fryers can also reduce the cooking time by 20% and temperature by 25 F on most oven recipes.

More meal choices

While they are air fryers, they can do much more than just cook typically fried food. With an air fryer, you can cook pre-fried frozen food such as fish sticks, chicken tenders, pizza rolls, and tater tots. Generally, portion-sized frozen foods and those that come in bite-size pieces can become crisp quickly when using an air fryer. An air fryer also lets you create from-scratch recipes similar to pre-fried frozen foods, such as air-fried chicken, crab cakes, air-fried mozzarella sticks, and more. Thinking of having baked potatoes and some chicken for dinner? It is possible to cook everything in an air fryer.

Less energy

Since air fryers are smaller than ovens, they can heat up faster, which means you can save energy and money. Unlike conventional ovens that require a long preheating time only for you to end up using a fraction of the available capacity, air fryers do not have a long preheating time. Furthermore, they come in various capacities to ensure that you use the available space as efficiently as possible.

Enough capacity

With an air fryer, you have a larger capacity than a toaster oven to cook your food. Furthermore, air fryers come in many different sizes and power ratings, so you can always be sure to find one that is sufficiently large to meet your cooking requirements.

Different Types of Air Fryers

There are various types of air fryers; while they all have the same underlying mechanics, their designs are slightly different.

Pressure cooker air fryer combos

A pressure cooker air fryer combo isn't as common as other types of air fryers on this list. However, they are designed to handle air frying and pressure-cooking on the same device. With this type of air fryer, you can utilise the pressure cooker functionality to thoroughly cook your meal, locking in the juices and flavours before using the air fryer function to crisp the outside.

Lid-type air fryer attachments

A lid-type air fryer is a type of air fryer that comes with an actual lid reminiscent of an instant pot or pressure cooker. This helps to thoroughly close the air fryer from the environment. These air fryers come with their own heating element inside the lid and a fan underneath. They were originally created to transform a non-air fryer into one.

Toaster oven air fryers

A toaster oven air fryer is perhaps one of the most popular air fryer types out there. It lets you do everything a typical air fryer can do and more. Some toaster oven air fryers let you dehydrate your meal as well as sear steaks.

This type of air fryer works and looks quite similar to a conventional oven—albeit with a running fan to move the air around—it can be a great air fryer to meet your needs. You should note that cleaning this air fryer is slightly more challenging than others since it comes with various components and a large chamber that requires a wipe-down. Nevertheless, the cleaning process is quick and simple.

Basket-type air fryers

The basket-style air fryer is what comes to the mind of most people when they think of an air fryer. This is because they are the most widely used air fryers found in numerous households. They are designed with a basket that can be pulled from the centre of the air fryer. The basket is typically constructed with non-stick coating and you can place a tray or grill underneath to catch all the fats and oils that drip from the basket.

Paddle-type air fryers

Paddle-type air fryers are probably the most interesting subcategory of air fryers. The design is peculiar, that resembles an upended frying pan. Nevertheless, you shouldn't let the design fool you, as it is one of the most capable air fryers out there. Just as with other types of air fryers, this one consists of a paddle and a bowl. The bowl continues to rotate your food, ensuring even cooking.

In a paddle-type air fryer, the middle part of the air fryer starts to spin on its end. This causes the food to stir, cooking it evenly and gently. This method helps you save time from having to flip and stir your food halfway through the cooking time.

Air Fryer Cooking Tips

Here are a few tips to consider when trying to cook with an air fryer:

You might need a slightly lower temperature

Many recipes might require a lower temperature than a conventional oven. The reason for this is that air fryers can get hot quite quickly and spread the heat evenly, so a slightly lower temperature can ensure your food doesn't get too crispy or dark on the outside while still getting cooked properly on the inside.

Get used to the faster cooking times.

One of the best attributes of an air fryer is that cooking times are a lot shorter than other cooking methods. You should thoroughly read your air fryer's manual to get a hand of the cooking temperatures and times for common food. Another tip to remember is the cooking time correlates to the amount of food in the basket. Less food equals shorter time.

Make sure the drawer is pushed all the way in

The last thing you want is to head out of the kitchen thinking your air fryer is on, only to discover that it isn't working because you didn't push your drawer in all the way. You will know your air fryer isn't working because it will be quiet.

Pulling the basket out to check your food is fine.

The design of an air fryer enables you to pull the basket out to check on your food while it is cooking. You don't have to worry about turning the air fryer off, as it stops cooking once you take the basket out.

Air fryers can be loud.

While the air fryer is running, you will notice that it can be quite loud. An air fryer uses fans to circulate the heat around your food, so you must deal with that.

Care And Cleaning

Regarding your air fryer, you cannot underestimate care and cleaning. You need to clean your air fryer after each use as failure to do so could result in a build-up of oil. This oil build-up can make your air fryer smoke. In certain instances, all you have to do is simply wipe the grate and drawer with a paper towel. You should hand wash these components if the grate and drawer are gunky. Fortunately, most models come with dishwasher-safe components, so check the manual to see if your air fryer is dishwasher-safe.

Air Fryer Q and A

Does an air fryer "fry" your food?

While it has the word "fryer" in its name, an air fryer doesn't fry your food. It uses dry heat to cook your food just as a conventional oven would.

Can I open the air fryer while cooking?

Yes you can open the air fryer while cooking, so long as the design of your air fryer allows you to do so. For instance, a paddle-type air fryer might not allow you to check on your food, where as a lid type, toaster oven, or basket-type might allow you to.

What type of cooking is an air fryer best suited for?

You can use your air fryer for all sorts of meals that require baking, frying, grilling, and roasting. An air fryer has many uses, to the point where you can cook vegetables with your air fryer. Furthermore, your air fryer can cook foods that require a light flour coating.

Meat lovers can utilise their air fryers to prepare chicken, beef, seafood, and fish. Vegetables such as asparagus, cauliflower, kale, peppers, and corn on the cob can be cooked using an air fryer. People that love baked goods can enjoy brownies, cakes, muffins, and garlic bread.

What types of food can you cook with an air fryer?

There are a plethora of foods you can make using an air fryer, including muffins, different variations of chicken and seafood, corn on the cob, potatoes and more.

Chapter 2 Breakfasts

Chapter 2 Breakfasts

Maple Granola

Prep time: 5 minutes | Cook time: 40 minutes | Makes 475 ml

235 ml rolled oats

3 tablespoons pure maple syrup

1 tablespoon sugar

1 tablespoon neutral-flavored oil, such as refined coconut or

sunflower

¼ teaspoon sea salt

¼ teaspoon ground cinnamon

¼ teaspoon vanilla extract

Insert the crisper plate into the basket and the basket into the unit. Preheat the unit by selecting BAKE, setting the temperature to 120°C, and setting the time to 3 minutes. Select START/STOP to begin.

In a medium bowl, stir together the oats, maple syrup, sugar, oil, salt, cinnamon, and vanilla until thoroughly combined. Transfer the granola to a 6-by-2-inch round baking pan.

Once the unit is preheated, place the pan into the basket.

Select BAKE, set the temperature to 120°C and set the time to 40 minutes. Select START/STOP to begin.

After 10 minutes, stir the granola well. Resume cooking, stirring the granola every 10 minutes, for a total of 40 minutes, or until the granola is lightly browned and mostly dry.

When the cooking is complete, place the granola on a plate to cool. It will become crisp as it cools. Store the completely cooled granola in an airtight container in a cool, dry place for 1 to 2 weeks.

Bacon, Egg, and Cheese Roll Ups

Prep time: 15 minutes | Cook time: 15 minutes | Serves 4

2 tablespoons unsalted butter

60 ml chopped onion

½ medium green pepper, seeded and chopped

6 large eggs

12 slices bacon

235 ml shredded sharp Cheddar cheese

120 ml mild salsa, for dipping

In a medium skillet over medium heat, melt butter. Add onion and pepper to the skillet and sauté until fragrant and onions are translucent, about 3 minutes.

Whisk eggs in a small bowl and pour into skillet. Scramble eggs with onions and peppers until fluffy and fully cooked, about 5 minutes. Remove from heat and set aside.

On work surface, place three slices of bacon side by side, overlapping about ¼ inch. Place 60 ml scrambled eggs in a heap on the side closest to you and sprinkle 60 ml cheese on top of the eggs. Tightly roll the bacon around the eggs and secure the seam with a toothpick if necessary. Place each roll into the air fryer basket.

Adjust the temperature to 176°C and air fry for 15 minutes. Rotate the rolls halfway through the cooking time.

Bacon will be brown and crispy when completely cooked. Serve immediately with salsa for dipping.

Breakfast Calzone

Prep time: 15 minutes | Cook time: 15 minutes | Serves 4

350 ml shredded Mozzarella cheese

120 ml blanched finely ground almond flour

30 g full-fat cream cheese

1 large whole egg

4 large eggs, scrambled

230 g cooked sausage meat, removed from casings and crumbled

8 tablespoons shredded mild Cheddar cheese

In a large microwave-safe bowl, add Mozzarella, almond flour, and cream cheese. Microwave for 1 minute. Stir until the mixture is smooth and forms a ball. Add the egg and stir until dough forms.

Place dough between two sheets of parchment and roll out to ¼-inch thickness. Cut the dough into four rectangles.

Mix scrambled eggs and cooked sausage together in a large bowl. Divide the mixture evenly among each piece of dough, placing it on the lower half of the rectangle. Sprinkle each with 2 tablespoons Cheddar.

Fold over the rectangle to cover the egg and meat mixture. Pinch, roll, or use a wet fork to close the edges completely.

Cut a piece of parchment to fit your air fryer basket and place the calzones onto the parchment. Place parchment into the air fryer basket.

Adjust the temperature to 192°C and air fry for 15 minutes.

Flip the calzones halfway through the cooking time. When done, calzones should be golden in color. Serve immediately.

Scotch Eggs

Prep time: 10 minutes | Cook time: 20 to 25 minutes | Serves 4

2 tablespoons flour, plus extra for coating

450 g sausage meat

4 hard-boiled eggs, peeled

1 raw egg

1 tablespoon water

Oil for misting or cooking spray

Crumb Coating:

180 ml panko bread crumbs

180 ml flour

Combine flour with sausage meat and mix thoroughly.

Divide into 4 equal portions and mold each around a hard-boiled egg so the sausage completely covers the egg.

In a small bowl, beat together the raw egg and water.

Dip sausage-covered eggs in the remaining flour, then the egg mixture, then roll in the crumb coating.

Air fry at 182°C for 10 minutes. Spray eggs, turn, and spray other side.

Continue cooking for another 10 to 15 minutes or until sausage is well done.

Apple Cider Doughnut Holes

Prep time: 10 minutes | Cook time: 6 minutes | Makes 10 mini doughnuts

Doughnut Holes:

350 ml plain flour

2 tablespoons granulated sugar

2 teaspoons baking powder

1 teaspoon baking soda

½ teaspoon coarse or flaky salt

Pinch of freshly grated nutmeg

60 ml plus 2 tablespoons buttermilk, chilled

2 tablespoons apple cider or

apple juice, chilled

1 large egg, lightly beaten

Vegetable oil, for brushing

Glaze:

120 ml icing sugar

2 tablespoons unsweetened applesauce

¼ teaspoon vanilla extract

Pinch of coarse or flaky salt

Make the doughnut holes: In a bowl, whisk together the flour, granulated sugar, baking powder, baking soda, salt, and nutmeg until smooth. Add the buttermilk, cider, and egg and stir with a small rubber spatula or spoon until the dough just comes together.

Using a 28 g ice cream scoop or 2 tablespoons, scoop and drop 10 balls of dough into the air fryer basket, spaced evenly apart, and brush the tops lightly with oil. Air fry at 176°C until the doughnut holes are golden brown and fluffy, about 6 minutes. Transfer the doughnut holes to a wire rack to cool completely.

Make the glaze: In a small bowl, stir together the powdered sugar, applesauce, vanilla, and salt until smooth.

Dip the tops of the doughnuts holes in the glaze, then let stand until the glaze sets before serving. If you're impatient and want warm doughnuts, have the glaze ready to go while the doughnuts cook, then use the glaze as a dipping sauce for the warm doughnuts, fresh out of the air fryer.

Veggie Frittata

Prep time: 7 minutes | Cook time: 21 to 23 minutes | Serves 2

Avocado oil spray

60 ml diced red onion

60 ml diced red pepper

60 ml finely chopped broccoli

4 large eggs

85 g shredded sharp Cheddar cheese, divided

½ teaspoon dried thyme

Sea salt and freshly ground black pepper, to taste

Spray a pan well with oil. Put the onion, pepper, and broccoli in the pan, place the pan in the air fryer, and set to 176°C. Bake for 5 minutes.

While the vegetables cook, beat the eggs in a medium bowl. Stir in half of the cheese, and season with the thyme, salt, and pepper.

Add the eggs to the pan and top with the remaining cheese. Set the air fryer to 176°C. Bake for 16 to 18 minutes, until cooked through.

Bacon and Spinach Egg Muffins

Prep time: 7 minutes | Cook time: 12 to 14 minutes | Serves 6

6 large eggs

60 ml double (whipping) cream

½ teaspoon sea salt

¼ teaspoon freshly ground black pepper

¼ teaspoon cayenne pepper

(optional)

180 ml frozen chopped spinach, thawed and drained

4 strips cooked bacon, crumbled

60 g shredded Cheddar cheese

In a large bowl (with a spout if you have one), whisk together the eggs, double cream, salt, black pepper, and cayenne pepper (if using).

Divide the spinach and bacon among 6 silicone muffin cups. Place the muffin cups in your air fryer basket.

Divide the egg mixture among the muffin cups. Top with the cheese.

Set the air fryer to 150°C. Bake for 12 to 14 minutes, until the eggs are set and cooked through.

Red Pepper and Feta Frittata

Prep time: 10 minutes | Cook time: 20 minutes | Serves 4

Olive oil cooking spray

8 large eggs

1 medium red pepper, diced

½ teaspoon salt

½ teaspoon black pepper

1 garlic clove, minced

120 ml feta, divided

Preheat the air fryer to 182ºC. Lightly coat the inside of a 6-inch round cake pan with olive oil cooking spray.

In a large bowl, beat the eggs for 1 to 2 minutes, or until well combined.

Add the red pepper, salt, black pepper, and garlic to the eggs, and mix together until the red pepper is distributed throughout.

Fold in 60 ml the feta cheese.

Pour the egg mixture into the prepared cake pan, and sprinkle the remaining 60 ml feta over the top.

Place into the air fryer and bake for 18 to 20 minutes, or until the eggs are set in the center.

Remove from the air fryer and allow to cool for 5 minutes before serving.

Green Eggs and Ham

Prep time: 5 minutes | Cook time: 10 minutes | Serves 2

1 large Hass avocado, halved and pitted

2 thin slices ham

2 large eggs

2 tablespoons chopped spring

onions, plus more for garnish

½ teaspoon fine sea salt

¼ teaspoon ground black pepper

60 ml shredded Cheddar cheese (omit for dairy-free)

Preheat the air fryer to 204ºC.

Place a slice of ham into the cavity of each avocado half. Crack an egg on top of the ham, then sprinkle on the green onions, salt, and pepper.

Place the avocado halves in the air fryer cut side up and air fry for 10 minutes, or until the egg is cooked to your desired doneness. Top with the cheese (if using) and air fry for 30 seconds more, or until the cheese is melted. Garnish with chopped green onions.

Best served fresh. Store extras in an airtight container in the fridge for up to 4 days. Reheat in a preheated 176ºC air fryer for a few minutes, until warmed through.

Breakfast Sausage and Cauliflower

Prep time: 5 minutes | Cook time: 45 minutes | Serves 4

450 g sausage meat, cooked and crumbled

475 ml double/whipping cream

1 head cauliflower, chopped

235 ml grated Cheddar cheese,

plus more for topping

8 eggs, beaten

Salt and ground black pepper, to taste

Preheat the air fryer to 176ºC.

In a large bowl, mix the sausage, cream, chopped cauliflower, cheese and eggs. Sprinkle with salt and ground black pepper.

Pour the mixture into a greased casserole dish. Bake in the preheated air fryer for 45 minutes or until firm.

Top with more Cheddar cheese and serve.

Turkey Breakfast Sausage Patties

Prep time: 5 minutes | Cook time: 10 minutes | Serves 4

1 tablespoon chopped fresh thyme

1 tablespoon chopped fresh sage

1¼ teaspoons coarse or flaky salt

1 teaspoon chopped fennel seeds

¾ teaspoon smoked paprika

½ teaspoon onion granules

½ teaspoon garlic powder

⅛ teaspoon crushed red pepper flakes

⅛ teaspoon freshly ground black pepper

450 g lean turkey mince

120 ml finely minced sweet apple (peeled)

Thoroughly combine the thyme, sage, salt, fennel seeds, paprika, onion granules, garlic powder, red pepper flakes, and black pepper in a medium bowl.

Add the turkey mince and apple and stir until well incorporated. Divide the mixture into 8 equal portions and shape into patties with your hands, each about ¼ inch thick and 3 inches in diameter.

Preheat the air fryer to 204ºC.

Place the patties in the air fryer basket in a single layer. You may need to work in batches to avoid overcrowding.

Air fry for 5 minutes. Flip the patties and air fry for 5 minutes, or until the patties are nicely browned and cooked through.

Remove from the basket to a plate and repeat with the remaining patties.

Serve warm.

Turkey Sausage Breakfast Pizza

Prep time: 15 minutes | Cook time: 24 minutes | Serves 2

4 large eggs, divided

1 tablespoon water

½ teaspoon garlic powder

½ teaspoon onion granules

½ teaspoon dried oregano

2 tablespoons coconut flour

3 tablespoons grated Parmesan cheese

120 ml shredded low-moisture Mozzarella or other melting cheese

1 link cooked turkey sausage, chopped (about 60 g)

2 sun-dried tomatoes, finely chopped

2 spring onions, thinly sliced

Preheat the air fryer to 204ºC. Line a cake pan with parchment paper and lightly coat the paper with olive oil.

In a large bowl, whisk 2 of the eggs with the water, garlic powder, onion granules, and dried oregano. Add the coconut flour, breaking up any lumps with your hands as you add it to the bowl. Stir the coconut flour into the egg mixture, mixing until smooth. Stir in the Parmesan cheese. Allow the mixture to rest for a few minutes until thick and dough-like.

Transfer the mixture to the prepared pan. Use a spatula to spread it evenly and slightly up the sides of the pan. Air fry until the crust is set but still light in color, about 10 minutes. Top with the cheeses, sausage, and sun-dried tomatoes.

Break the remaining 2 eggs into a small bowl, then slide them onto the pizza. Return the pizza to the air fryer. Air fry 10 to 14 minutes until the egg whites are set and the yolks are the desired doneness. Top with the scallions and allow to rest for 5 minutes before serving.

Simple Cinnamon Toasts

Prep time: 5 minutes | Cook time: 4 minutes | Serves 4

1 tablespoon salted butter

2 teaspoons ground cinnamon

4 tablespoons sugar

½ teaspoon vanilla extract

10 bread slices

Preheat the air fryer to 192ºC.

In a bowl, combine the butter, cinnamon, sugar, and vanilla extract. Spread onto the slices of bread.

Put the bread inside the air fryer and bake for 4 minutes or until golden brown.

Serve warm.

Cheddar Soufflés

Prep time: 15 minutes | Cook time: 12 minutes | Serves 4

3 large eggs, whites and yolks separated

¼ teaspoon cream of tartar

120 ml shredded sharp Cheddar cheese

85 g cream cheese, softened

In a large bowl, beat egg whites together with cream of tartar until soft peaks form, about 2 minutes.

In a separate medium bowl, beat egg yolks, Cheddar, and cream cheese together until frothy, about 1 minute. Add egg yolk mixture to whites, gently folding until combined.

Pour mixture evenly into four ramekins greased with cooking spray. Place ramekins into air fryer basket. Adjust the temperature to 176ºC and bake for 12 minutes. Eggs will be browned on the top and firm in the center when done. Serve warm.

Mushroom-and-Tomato Stuffed Hash Browns

Prep time: 10 minutes | Cook time: 20 minutes | Serves 4

Olive oil cooking spray

1 tablespoon plus 2 teaspoons olive oil, divided

110 g baby mushrooms, diced

1 spring onion, white parts and green parts, diced

1 garlic clove, minced

475 ml shredded potatoes

½ teaspoon salt

¼ teaspoon black pepper

1 plum tomato, diced

120 ml shredded mozzarella

Preheat the air fryer to 192ºC. Lightly coat the inside of a 6-inch cake pan with olive oil cooking spray.

In a small skillet, heat 2 teaspoons olive oil over medium heat. Add the mushrooms, spring onion, and garlic, and cook for 4 to 5 minutes, or until they have softened and are beginning to show some color. Remove from heat.

Meanwhile, in a large bowl, combine the potatoes, salt, pepper, and the remaining tablespoon olive oil. Toss until all potatoes are well coated.

Pour half of the potatoes into the bottom of the cake pan. Top with the mushroom mixture, tomato, and mozzarella. Spread the remaining potatoes over the top.

Bake in the air fryer for 12 to 15 minutes, or until the top is golden brown.

Remove from the air fryer and allow to cool for 5 minutes before slicing and serving.

Onion Omelette

Prep time: 10 minutes | Cook time: 12 minutes | Serves 2

3 eggs	1 large onion, chopped
Salt and ground black pepper, to taste	2 tablespoons grated Cheddar cheese
½ teaspoons soy sauce	Cooking spray

Preheat the air fryer to 180ºC.

In a bowl, whisk together the eggs, salt, pepper, and soy sauce.

Spritz a small pan with cooking spray. Spread the chopped onion across the bottom of the pan, then transfer the pan to the air fryer.

Bake in the preheated air fryer for 6 minutes or until the onion is translucent.

Add the egg mixture on top of the onions to coat well. Add the cheese on top, then continue baking for another 6 minutes.

Allow to cool before serving.

Hearty Cheddar Biscuits

Prep time: 10 minutes | Cook time: 22 minutes | Makes 8 biscuits

550 ml self-raising flour	plus more to melt on top
2 tablespoons sugar	315 ml buttermilk
120 ml butter, frozen for 15 minutes	235 ml plain flour, for shaping
120 ml grated Cheddar cheese,	1 tablespoon butter, melted

Line a buttered 7-inch metal cake pan with parchment paper or a silicone liner.

Combine the flour and sugar in a large mixing bowl. Grate the butter into the flour. Add the grated cheese and stir to coat the cheese and butter with flour. Then add the buttermilk and stir just until you can no longer see streaks of flour. The dough should be quite wet.

Spread the plain (not self-raising) flour out on a small cookie sheet. With a spoon, scoop 8 evenly sized balls of dough into the flour, making sure they don't touch each other. With floured hands, coat each dough ball with flour and toss them gently from hand to hand to shake off any excess flour. Put each floured dough ball into the prepared pan, right up next to the other. This will help the biscuits rise, rather than spreading out.

Preheat the air fryer to 192ºC.

Transfer the cake pan to the basket of the air fryer. Let the ends of the aluminum foil sling hang across the cake pan before returning the basket to the air fryer.

Air fry for 20 minutes. Check the biscuits twice to make sure they are not getting too brown on top. If they are, re-arrange the aluminum foil strips to cover any brown parts. After 20 minutes, check the biscuits by inserting a toothpick into the center of the biscuits. It should come out clean. If it needs a little more time, continue to air fry for two extra minutes. Brush the tops of the biscuits with some melted butter and sprinkle a little more grated cheese on top if desired. Pop the basket back into the air fryer for another 2 minutes.

Remove the cake pan from the air fryer. Let the biscuits cool for just a minute or two and then turn them out onto a plate and pull apart. Serve immediately.

Greek Bagels

Prep time: 10 minutes | Cook time: 10 minutes | Makes 2 bagels

120 ml self-raising flour, plus more for dusting	4 teaspoons sesame seeds or za'atar
120 ml plain Greek yoghurt	Cooking oil spray
1 egg	1 tablespoon butter, melted
1 tablespoon water	

In a large bowl, using a wooden spoon, stir together the flour and yoghurt until a tacky dough forms. Transfer the dough to a lightly floured work surface and roll the dough into a ball.

Cut the dough into 2 pieces and roll each piece into a log. Form each log into a bagel shape, pinching the ends together.

In a small bowl, whisk the egg and water. Brush the egg wash on the bagels.

Sprinkle 2 teaspoons of the toppings on each bagel and gently press it into the dough.

Insert the crisper plate into the basket and the basket into the unit. Preheat the unit by selecting BAKE, setting the temperature to 166ºC, and setting the time to 3 minutes. Select START/STOP to begin.

Once the unit is preheated, spray the crisper plate with cooking spray. Drizzle the bagels with the butter and place them into the basket.

Select BAKE, set the temperature to 166ºC, and set the time to 10 minutes. Select START/STOP to begin.

When the cooking is complete, the bagels should be lightly golden on the outside. Serve warm.

Everything Bagels

Prep time: 15 minutes | Cook time: 14 minutes | Makes 6 bagels

415 ml shredded Mozzarella cheese or goat cheese Mozzarella

2 tablespoons unsalted butter or coconut oil

1 large egg, beaten

1 tablespoon apple cider vinegar

235 ml blanched almond flour

1 tablespoon baking powder

⅛ teaspoon fine sea salt

1½ teaspoons sesame seeds or za'atar

Make the dough: Put the Mozzarella and butter in a large microwave-safe bowl and microwave for 1 to 2 minutes, until the cheese is entirely melted. Stir well. Add the egg and vinegar. Using a hand mixer on medium, combine well. Add the almond flour, baking powder, and salt and, using the mixer, combine well.

Lay a piece of parchment paper on the countertop and place the dough on it. Knead it for about 3 minutes. The dough should be a little sticky but pliable. (If the dough is too sticky, chill it in the refrigerator for an hour or overnight.)

Preheat the air fryer to 176ºC. Spray a baking sheet or pie pan that will fit into your air fryer with avocado oil.

Divide the dough into 6 equal portions. Roll 1 portion into a log that is 6 inches long and about ½ inch thick. Form the log into a circle and seal the edges together, making a bagel shape. Repeat with the remaining portions of dough, making 6 bagels.

Place the bagels on the greased baking sheet. Spray the bagels with avocado oil and top with everything bagel seasoning, pressing the seasoning into the dough with your hands.

Place the bagels in the air fryer and bake for 14 minutes, or until cooked through and golden brown, flipping after 6 minutes.

Remove the bagels from the air fryer and allow them to cool slightly before slicing them in half and serving. Store leftovers in an airtight container in the fridge for up to 4 days or in the freezer for up to a month.

Berry Muffins

Prep time: 15 minutes | Cook time: 12 to 17 minutes | Makes 8 muffins

315 ml plus 1 tablespoon plain flour, divided

60 ml granulated sugar

2 tablespoons light brown sugar

2 teaspoons baking powder

2 eggs

160 ml whole milk

80 ml neutral oil

235 ml mixed fresh berries

In a medium bowl, stir together 315 ml of flour, the granulated sugar, brown sugar, and baking powder until mixed well.

In a small bowl, whisk the eggs, milk, and oil until combined. Stir the egg mixture into the dry ingredients just until combined.

In another small bowl, toss the mixed berries with the remaining 1 tablespoon of flour until coated. Gently stir the berries into the batter.

Double up 16 foil muffin cups to make 8 cups.

Insert the crisper plate into the basket and the basket into the unit. Preheat the unit by selecting BAKE, setting the temperature to 156ºC, and setting the time to 3 minutes. Select START/STOP to begin.

Once the unit is preheated, place 1 L into the basket and fill each three-quarters full with the batter.

Select BAKE, set the temperature to 156ºC, and set the time for 17 minutes. Select START/STOP to begin.

After about 12 minutes, check the muffins. If they spring back when lightly touched with your finger, they are done. If not, resume cooking.

When the cooking is done, transfer the muffins to a wire rack to cool. 10. Repeat steps 6, 7, and 8 with the remaining muffin cups and batter. 1Let the muffins cool for 10 minutes before serving.

Chapter 3 Snacks and Appetizers

Chapter 3 Snacks and Appetizers

Ranch Oyster Snack Crackers

Prep time: 3 minutes | Cook time: 12 minutes | Serves 6

Oil, for spraying
60 ml olive oil
2 teaspoons dry ranch seasoning
1 teaspoon chilli powder
½ teaspoon dried dill
½ teaspoon granulated garlic
½ teaspoon salt
1 (255 g) bag oyster crackers or low-salt crackers

Preheat the air fryer to 164ºC. Line the air fryer basket with parchment and spray lightly with oil.

In a large bowl, mix together the olive oil, ranch seasoning, chilli powder, dill, garlic, and salt. Add the crackers and toss until evenly coated.

Place the mixture in the prepared basket.

Cook for 10 to 12 minutes, shaking or stirring every 3 to 4 minutes, or until crisp and golden brown.

Spicy Tortilla Chips

Prep time: 5 minutes | Cook time: 8 to 12 minutes | Serves 4

½ teaspoon ground cumin
½ teaspoon paprika
½ teaspoon chilli powder
½ teaspoon salt
Pinch cayenne pepper
8 (6-inch) corn tortillas, each cut into 6 wedges
Cooking spray

Preheat the air fryer to 192ºC. Lightly spritz the air fryer basket with cooking spray.

Stir together the cumin, paprika, chilli powder, salt, and pepper in a small bowl.

Working in batches, arrange the tortilla wedges in the air fryer basket in a single layer. Lightly mist them with cooking spray. Sprinkle some seasoning mixture on top of the tortilla wedges.

Air fry for 4 to 6 minutes, shaking the basket halfway through, or until the chips are lightly browned and crunchy.

Repeat with the remaining tortilla wedges and seasoning mixture.

Let the tortilla chips cool for 5 minutes and serve.

Garlic-Parmesan Croutons

Prep time: 3 minutes | Cook time: 12 minutes | Serves 4

Oil, for spraying
1 L cubed French bread
1 tablespoon grated Parmesan cheese
3 tablespoons olive oil
1 tablespoon granulated garlic
½ teaspoon unsalted salt

Line the air fryer basket with parchment and spray lightly with oil. In a large bowl, mix together the bread, Parmesan cheese, olive oil, garlic, and salt, tossing with your hands to evenly distribute the seasonings. Transfer the coated bread cubes to the prepared basket. Air fry at 176ºC for 10 to 12 minutes, stirring once after 5 minutes, or until crisp and golden brown.

Shishito Peppers with Herb Dressing

Prep time: 10 minutes | Cook time: 6 minutes | Serves 2 to 4

170 g shishito or Padron peppers
1 tablespoon vegetable oil
Rock salt and freshly ground black pepper, to taste
120 ml mayonnaise
2 tablespoons finely chopped fresh basil leaves
2 tablespoons finely chopped
fresh flat-leaf parsley
1 tablespoon finely chopped fresh tarragon
1 tablespoon finely chopped fresh chives
Finely grated zest of ½ lemon
1 tablespoon fresh lemon juice
Flaky sea salt, for serving

Preheat the air fryer to 204ºC.

In a bowl, toss together the shishitos and oil to evenly coat and season with rock salt and black pepper. Transfer to the air fryer and air fry for 6 minutes, shaking the basket halfway through, or until the shishitos are blistered and lightly charred.

Meanwhile, in a small bowl, whisk together the mayonnaise, basil, parsley, tarragon, chives, lemon zest, and lemon juice.

Pile the peppers on a plate, sprinkle with flaky sea salt, and serve hot with the dressing.

Crunchy Tex-Mex Tortilla Chips

Prep time: 5 minutes | Cook time: 5 minutes | Serves 4

Olive oil

½ teaspoon salt

½ teaspoon ground cumin

½ teaspoon chilli powder

½ teaspoon paprika

Pinch cayenne pepper

8 (6-inch) corn tortillas, each cut into 6 wedges

Spray fryer basket lightly with olive oil.

In a small bowl, combine the salt, cumin, chilli powder, paprika, and cayenne pepper.

Place the tortilla wedges in the air fryer basket in a single layer. Spray the tortillas lightly with oil and sprinkle with some of the seasoning mixture. You will need to cook the tortillas in batches.

Air fry at 192ºC for 2 to 3 minutes. Shake the basket and cook until the chips are light brown and crispy, an additional 2 to 3 minutes. Watch the chips closely so they do not burn.

Spiralized Potato Nest with Tomato Ketchup

Prep time: 10 minutes | Cook time: 15 minutes | Serves 2

1 large russet or Maris Piper potato (about 340 g)

2 tablespoons vegetable oil

1 tablespoon hot smoked paprika

½ teaspoon garlic powder

Rock salt and freshly ground black pepper, to taste

120 ml canned crushed tomatoes

2 tablespoons apple cider vinegar

1 tablespoon dark brown sugar

1 tablespoon Worcestershire sauce

1 teaspoon mild hot sauce

Using a spiralizer, spiralize the potato, then place in a large colander. (If you don't have a spiralizer, cut the potato into thin ⅛-inch-thick matchsticks.) Rinse the potatoes under cold running water until the water runs clear. Spread the potatoes out on a double-thick layer of paper towels and pat completely dry.

In a large bowl, combine the potatoes, oil, paprika, and garlic powder. Season with salt and pepper and toss to combine. Transfer the potatoes to the air fryer and air fry at 204ºC until the potatoes are browned and crisp, 15 minutes, shaking the basket halfway through.

Meanwhile, in a small blender, purée the tomatoes, vinegar, brown sugar, Worcestershire, and hot sauce until smooth. Pour into a small saucepan or skillet and simmer over medium heat until reduced by half, 3 to 5 minutes. Pour the homemade ketchup into a bowl and let cool.

Remove the spiralized potato nest from the air fryer and serve hot with the ketchup.

Cheesy Steak Fries

Prep time: 5 minutes | Cook time: 20 minutes | Serves 5

1 (794 g) bag frozen steak fries

Cooking spray

Salt and pepper, to taste

120 ml beef gravy

240 ml shredded Mozzarella cheese

2 spring onions, green parts only, chopped

Preheat the air fryer to 204ºC.

Place the frozen steak fries in the air fryer. Air fry for 10 minutes. Shake the basket and spritz the fries with cooking spray. Sprinkle with salt and pepper. Air fry for an additional 8 minutes.

Pour the beef gravy into a medium, microwave-safe bowl. Microwave for 30 seconds, or until the gravy is warm.

Sprinkle the fries with the cheese. Air fry for an additional 2 minutes, until the cheese is melted.

Transfer the fries to a serving dish. Drizzle the fries with gravy and sprinkle the spring onions on top for a green garnish. Serve.

Greek Yoghurt Devilled Eggs

Prep time: 15 minutes | Cook time: 15 minutes | Serves 4

4 eggs

60 ml non-fat plain Greek yoghurt

1 teaspoon chopped fresh dill

⅛ teaspoon salt

⅛ teaspoon paprika

⅛ teaspoon garlic powder

Chopped fresh parsley, for garnish

Preheat the air fryer to 127ºC.

Place the eggs in a single layer in the air fryer basket and cook for 15 minutes.

Quickly remove the eggs from the air fryer and place them into a cold water bath. Let the eggs cool in the water for 10 minutes before removing and peeling them.

After peeling the eggs, cut them in half.

Spoon the yolk into a small bowl. Add the yoghurt, dill, salt, paprika, and garlic powder and mix until smooth.

Spoon or pipe the yolk mixture into the halved egg whites. Serve with a sprinkle of fresh parsley on top.

Egg Roll Pizza Sticks

Prep time: 10 minutes | Cook time: 5 minutes | Serves 4

Olive oil

8 pieces low-fat string cheese

8 egg roll wrappers or spring roll pastry

24 slices turkey pepperoni or salami

Marinara sauce, for dipping (optional)

Spray the air fryer basket lightly with olive oil. Fill a small bowl with water.

Place each egg roll wrapper diagonally on a work surface. It should look like a diamond.

Place 3 slices of turkey pepperoni in a vertical line down the centre of the wrapper.

Place 1 Mozzarella cheese stick on top of the turkey pepperoni.

Fold the top and bottom corners of the egg roll wrapper over the cheese stick.

Fold the left corner over the cheese stick and roll the cheese stick up to resemble a spring roll. Dip a finger in the water and seal the edge of the roll

Repeat with the rest of the pizza sticks.

Place them in the air fryer basket in a single layer, making sure to leave a little space between each one. Lightly spray the pizza sticks with oil. You may need to cook these in batches.

Air fry at 192ºC until the pizza sticks are lightly browned and crispy, about 5 minutes. 10. These are best served hot while the cheese is melted. Accompany with a small bowl of marinara sauce, if desired.

Pork and Cabbage Egg Rolls

Prep time: 15 minutes | Cook time: 12 minutes | Makes 12 egg rolls

Cooking oil spray

2 garlic cloves, minced

340 g minced pork

1 teaspoon sesame oil

60 ml soy sauce

2 teaspoons grated peeled fresh

ginger

475 ml shredded green cabbage

4 spring onions, green parts (white parts optional), chopped

24 egg roll wrappers

Spray a skillet with the cooking oil and place it over medium-high heat. Add the garlic and cook for 1 minute until fragrant.

Add the minced pork to the skillet. Using a spoon, break the pork into smaller chunks.

In a small bowl, whisk the sesame oil, soy sauce, and ginger until combined. Add the sauce to the skillet. Stir to combine and continue cooking for about 5 minutes until the pork is browned and thoroughly cooked.

Stir in the cabbage and spring onions. Transfer the pork mixture to a large bowl.

Lay the egg roll wrappers on a flat surface. Dip a basting brush in water and glaze each egg roll wrapper along the edges with the wet brush. This will soften the dough and make it easier to roll.

Stack 2 egg roll wrappers (it works best if you double-wrap the egg rolls). Scoop 1 to 2 tablespoons of the pork mixture into the centre of each wrapper stack.

Roll one long side of the wrappers up over the filling. Press firmly on the area with the filling, tucking it in lightly to secure it in place. Fold in the left and right sides. Continue rolling to close. Use the basting brush to wet the seam and seal the egg roll. Repeat with the remaining ingredients.

Insert the crisper plate into the basket and the basket into the unit. Preheat the unit by selecting AIR FRY, setting the temperature to 204ºC, and setting the time to 3 minutes. Select START/STOP to begin.

Once the unit is preheated, spray the crisper plate with cooking oil. Place the egg rolls into the basket. It is okay to stack them. Spray them with cooking oil. 10. Select AIR FRY, set the temperature to 204ºC, and set the time to 12 minutes. Insert the basket into the unit. Select START/STOP to begin. 1After 8 minutes, use tongs to flip the egg rolls. Reinsert the basket to resume cooking. 12. When the cooking is complete, serve the egg rolls hot.

Crispy Breaded Beef Cubes

Prep time: 10 minutes | Cook time: 12 to 16 minutes | Serves 4

450 g sirloin tip, cut into 1-inch cubes

240 ml cheese pasta sauce

355 ml soft breadcrumbs

2 tablespoons olive oil

½ teaspoon dried marjoram

Preheat the air fryer to 182ºC.

In a medium bowl, toss the beef with the pasta sauce to coat.

In a shallow bowl, combine the breadcrumbs, oil, and marjoram, and mix well. Drop the beef cubes, one at a time, into the bread crumb mixture to coat thoroughly.

Air fry the beef in two batches for 6 to 8 minutes, shaking the basket once during cooking time, until the beef is at least 63ºC and the outside is crisp and brown.

Serve hot.

Polenta Fries with Chilli-Lime Mayo

Prep time: 10 minutes | Cook time: 28 minutes | Serves 4

Polenta Fries:

2 teaspoons vegetable or olive oil

¼ teaspoon paprika

450 g prepared polenta, cut into 3-inch × ½-inch strips

Chilli-Lime Mayo:

120 ml mayonnaise

1 teaspoon chilli powder

1 teaspoon chopped fresh coriander

¼ teaspoon ground cumin

Juice of ½ lime

Salt and freshly ground black pepper, to taste

Preheat the air fryer to 204ºC.

Mix the oil and paprika in a bowl. Add the polenta strips and toss until evenly coated.

Transfer the polenta strips to the air fry basket and air fry for 28 minutes until the fries are golden brown, shaking the basket once during cooking. Season as desired with salt and pepper.

Meanwhile, whisk together all the ingredients for the chilli-lime mayo in a small bowl.

Remove the polenta fries from the air fryer to a plate and serve alongside the chilli-lime mayo as a dipping sauce.

Authentic Scotch Eggs

Prep time: 15 minutes | Cook time: 11 to 13 minutes | Serves 6

680 g bulk lean chicken or turkey sausage

3 raw eggs, divided

355 ml dried breadcrumbs,

divided

120 ml plain flour

6 hardboiled eggs, peeled

Cooking oil spray

In a large bowl, combine the chicken sausage, 1 raw egg, and 120 ml of breadcrumbs and mix well. Divide the mixture into 6 pieces and flatten each into a long oval.

In a shallow bowl, beat the remaining 2 raw eggs.

Place the flour in a small bowl.

Place the remaining 240 ml of breadcrumbs in a second small bowl.

Roll each hardboiled egg in the flour and wrap one of the chicken sausage pieces around each egg to encircle it completely.

One at a time, roll the encased eggs in the flour, dip in the beaten eggs, and finally dip in the breadcrumbs to coat.

Insert the crisper plate into the basket and the basket into the unit.

Preheat the unit by selecting AIR FRY, setting the temperature to 192ºC, and setting the time to 3 minutes. Select START/STOP to begin.

Once the unit is preheated, spray the crisper plate with cooking oil. Place the eggs in a single layer into the basket and spray them with oil.

Select AIR FRY, set the temperature to 192ºC, and set the time to 13 minutes. Select START/STOP to begin. 10. After about 6 minutes, use tongs to turn the eggs and spray them with more oil. Resume cooking for 5 to 7 minutes more, or until the chicken is thoroughly cooked and the Scotch eggs are browned. 1When the cooking is complete, serve warm.

Cheese Drops

Prep time: 15 minutes | Cook time: 10 minutes per batch | Serves 8

177 ml plain flour

½ teaspoon rock salt

¼ teaspoon cayenne pepper

¼ teaspoon smoked paprika

¼ teaspoon black pepper

Dash garlic powder (optional)

60 ml butter, softened

240 ml shredded extra mature Cheddar cheese, at room temperature

Olive oil spray

In a small bowl, combine the flour, salt, cayenne, paprika, pepper, and garlic powder, if using.

Using a food processor, cream the butter and cheese until smooth. Gently add the seasoned flour and process until the dough is well combined, smooth, and no longer sticky. (Or make the dough in a stand mixer fitted with the paddle attachment: Cream the butter and cheese on medium speed until smooth, then add the seasoned flour and beat at low speed until smooth.)

Divide the dough into 32 equal-size pieces. On a lightly floured surface, roll each piece into a small ball.

Spray the air fryer basket with oil spray. Arrange 16 cheese drops in the basket. Set the air fryer to 164ºC for 10 minutes, or until drops are just starting to brown. Transfer to a wire rack. Repeat with remaining dough, checking for doneness at 8 minutes.

Cool the cheese drops completely on the wire rack. Store in an airtight container until ready to serve, or up to 1 or 2 days.

Crispy Filo Artichoke Triangles

Prep time: 15 minutes | Cook time: 9 to 12 minutes | Makes 18 triangles

60 ml Ricotta cheese

1 egg white

80 ml minced and drained artichoke hearts

3 tablespoons grated Mozzarella

cheese

½ teaspoon dried thyme

6 sheets frozen filo pastry, thawed

2 tablespoons melted butter

Preheat the air fryer to 204°C.

In a small bowl, combine the Ricotta cheese, egg white, artichoke hearts, Mozzarella cheese, and thyme, and mix well.

Cover the filo pastry with a damp kitchen towel while you work so it doesn't dry out. Using one sheet at a time, place on the work surface and cut into thirds lengthwise.

Put about 1½ teaspoons of the filling on each strip at the base. Fold the bottom right-hand tip of phyllo over the filling to meet the other side in a triangle, then continue folding in a triangle. Brush each triangle with butter to seal the edges. Repeat with the remaining phyllo dough and filling.

Place the triangles in the air fryer basket. Bake, 6 at a time, for about 3 to 4 minutes, or until the filo is golden brown and crisp. Serve hot.

Spinach and Crab Meat Cups

Prep time: 10 minutes | Cook time: 10 minutes | Makes 30 cups

1 (170 g) can crab meat, drained to yield 80 ml meat

60 ml frozen spinach, thawed, drained, and chopped

1 clove garlic, minced

120 ml grated Parmesan cheese

3 tablespoons plain yoghurt

¼ teaspoon lemon juice

½ teaspoon Worcestershire sauce

30 mini frozen filo shells, thawed

Cooking spray

Preheat the air fryer to 200°C.

Remove any bits of shell that might remain in the crab meat.

Mix the crab meat, spinach, garlic, and cheese together.

Stir in the yoghurt, lemon juice, and Worcestershire sauce and mix well.

Spoon a teaspoon of filling into each filo shell.

Spray the air fryer basket with cooking spray and arrange half the shells in the basket. Air fry for 5 minutes. Repeat with the remaining shells.

Serve immediately.

Vegetable Pot Stickers

Prep time: 12 minutes | Cook time: 11 to 18 minutes | Makes 12 pot stickers

240 ml shredded red cabbage

60 ml chopped button mushrooms

60 ml grated carrot

2 tablespoons minced onion

2 garlic cloves, minced

2 teaspoons grated fresh ginger

12 gyoza/pot sticker wrappers

2½ teaspoons olive oil, divided

In a baking pan, combine the red cabbage, mushrooms, carrot, onion, garlic, and ginger. Add 1 tablespoon of water. Place in the air fryer and air fry at 188°C for 3 to 6 minutes, until the vegetables are crisp-tender. Drain and set aside.

Working one at a time, place the pot sticker wrappers on a work surface. Top each wrapper with a scant 1 tablespoon of the filling. Fold half of the wrapper over the other half to form a half circle. Dab one edge with water and press both edges together.

To another pan, add 1¼ teaspoons of olive oil. Put half of the pot stickers, seam-side up, in the pan. Air fry for 5 minutes, or until the bottoms are light golden brown. Add 1 tablespoon of water and return the pan to the air fryer.

Air fry for 4 to 6 minutes more, or until hot. Repeat with the remaining pot stickers, remaining 1¼ teaspoons of oil, and another tablespoon of water. Serve immediately.

Artichoke and Olive Pitta Flatbread

Prep time: 5 minutes | Cook time: 10 minutes | Serves 4

2 wholewheat pittas

2 tablespoons olive oil, divided

2 garlic cloves, minced

¼ teaspoon salt

120 ml canned artichoke hearts,

sliced

60 ml Kalamata olives

60 ml shredded Parmesan

60 ml crumbled feta

Chopped fresh parsley, for garnish (optional)

Preheat the air fryer to 192°C.

Brush each pitta with 1 tablespoon olive oil, then sprinkle the minced garlic and salt over the top.

Distribute the artichoke hearts, olives, and cheeses evenly between the two pittas, and place both into the air fryer to bake for 10 minutes.

Remove the pittas and cut them into 4 pieces each before serving. Sprinkle parsley over the top, if desired.

Crispy Mozzarella Sticks

Prep time: 8 minutes | Cook time: 5 minutes | Serves 4

120 ml plain flour

1 egg, beaten

120 ml panko breadcrumbs

120 ml grated Parmesan cheese

1 teaspoon Italian seasoning

½ teaspoon garlic salt

6 Mozzarella sticks, halved crosswise

Olive oil spray

Put the flour in a small bowl.

Put the beaten egg in another small bowl.

In a medium bowl, stir together the panko, Parmesan cheese, Italian seasoning, and garlic salt.

Roll a Mozzarella-stick half in the flour, dip it into the egg, and then roll it in the panko mixture to coat. Press the coating lightly to make sure the breadcrumbs stick to the cheese. Repeat with the remaining 11 Mozzarella sticks.

Insert the crisper plate into the basket and the basket into the unit. Preheat the unit by selecting AIR FRY, setting the temperature to 204°C, and setting the time to 3 minutes. Select START/STOP to begin.

Once the unit is preheated, spray the crisper plate with olive oil and place a parchment paper liner in the basket. Place the Mozzarella sticks into the basket and lightly spray them with olive oil.

Select AIR FRY, set the temperature to 204°C, and set the time to 5 minutes. Select START/STOP to begin.

When the cooking is complete, the Mozzarella sticks should be golden and crispy. Let the sticks stand for 1 minute before transferring them to a serving plate. Serve warm.

Roasted Pearl Onion Dip

Prep time: 5 minutes | Cook time: 12 minutes | Serves 4

475 ml peeled pearl onions

3 garlic cloves

3 tablespoons olive oil, divided

½ teaspoon salt

240 ml non-fat plain Greek yoghurt

1 tablespoon lemon juice

¼ teaspoon black pepper

⅛ teaspoon red pepper flakes

Pitta chips, vegetables, or toasted bread for serving (optional)

Preheat the air fryer to 182°C.

In a large bowl, combine the pearl onions and garlic with 2 tablespoons of the olive oil until the onions are well coated.

Pour the garlic-and-onion mixture into the air fryer basket and roast for 12 minutes.

Transfer the garlic and onions to a food processor. Pulse the vegetables several times, until the onions are minced but still have some chunks.

In a large bowl, combine the garlic and onions and the remaining 1 tablespoon of olive oil, along with the salt, yoghurt, lemon juice, black pepper, and red pepper flakes.

Cover and chill for 1 hour before serving with pitta chips, vegetables, or toasted bread.

Chapter 4 Vegetables and Sides

Chapter 4 Vegetables and Sides

Parmesan Mushrooms

Prep time: 5 minutes | Cook time: 15 minutes | Serves 4

Oil, for spraying

450 g shitake mushrooms, stems trimmed

2 tablespoons olive oil

2 teaspoons granulated garlic

1 teaspoon onion powder

½ teaspoon salt

¼ teaspoon freshly ground black pepper

30 g grated Parmesan cheese, divided

Line the air fryer basket with parchment and spray lightly with oil.

In a large bowl, toss the mushrooms with the olive oil, garlic, onion powder, salt, and black pepper until evenly coated.

Place the mushrooms in the prepared basket.

Roast at 192°C for 13 minutes.

Sprinkle half of the cheese over the mushrooms and cook for another 2 minutes.

Transfer the mushrooms to a serving bowl, add the remaining Parmesan cheese, and toss until evenly coated. Serve immediately.

Maple-Roasted Tomatoes

Prep time: 15 minutes | Cook time: 20 minutes | Serves 2

280 g cherry tomatoes, halved

coarse sea salt, to taste

2 tablespoons maple syrup

1 tablespoon vegetable oil

2 sprigs fresh thyme, stems removed

1 garlic clove, minced

Freshly ground black pepper

Place the tomatoes in a colander and sprinkle liberally with salt. Let stand for 10 minutes to drain.

Transfer the tomatoes cut-side up to a cake pan, then drizzle with the maple syrup, followed by the oil. Sprinkle with the thyme leaves and garlic and season with pepper. Place the pan in the air fryer and roast at 160°C until the tomatoes are soft, collapsed, and lightly caramelized on top, about 20 minutes.

Serve straight from the pan or transfer the tomatoes to a plate and drizzle with the juices from the pan to serve.

Polenta Casserole

Prep time: 5 minutes | Cook time: 28 to 30 minutes | Serves 4

10 fresh asparagus spears, cut into 1-inch pieces

320 g cooked polenta, cooled to room temperature

1 egg, beaten

2 teaspoons Worcestershire

sauce

½ teaspoon garlic powder

¼ teaspoon salt

2 slices emmental cheese (about 40 g)

Oil for misting or cooking spray

Mist asparagus spears with oil and air fry at 200°C for 5 minutes, until crisp-tender.

In a medium bowl, mix together the grits, egg, Worcestershire, garlic powder, and salt.

Spoon half of polenta mixture into a baking pan and top with asparagus.

Tear cheese slices into pieces and layer evenly on top of asparagus.

Top with remaining polenta.

Bake at 180°C for 23 to 25 minutes. The casserole will rise a little as it cooks. When done, the top will have browned lightly with just a hint of crispiness.

Roasted Brussels Sprouts with Bacon

Prep time: 10 minutes | Cook time: 20 minutes | Serves 4

4 slices thick-cut bacon, chopped (about 110 g)

450 g Brussels sprouts, halved

(or quartered if large)

Freshly ground black pepper, to taste

Preheat the air fryer to 192°C.

Air fry the bacon for 5 minutes, shaking the basket once or twice during the cooking time.

Add the Brussels sprouts to the basket and drizzle a little bacon fat from the bottom of the air fryer drawer into the basket. Toss the sprouts to coat with the bacon fat. Air fry for an additional 15 minutes, or until the Brussels sprouts are tender to a knifepoint.

Season with freshly ground black pepper.

Buttery Mushrooms

Prep time: 10 minutes | Cook time: 10 minutes | Serves 4

230 g shitake mushrooms, halved	melted
	¼ teaspoon salt
2 tablespoons salted butter,	¼ teaspoon ground black pepper

In a medium bowl, toss mushrooms with butter, then sprinkle with salt and pepper. Place into ungreased air fryer basket. Adjust the temperature to 200°Cand air fry for 10 minutes, shaking the basket halfway through cooking. Mushrooms will be tender when done. Serve warm.

Mexican Corn in a Cup

Prep time: 5 minutes | Cook time: 10 minutes | Serves 4

650 g frozen corn kernels (do not thaw)	2 tablespoons fresh lemon or lime juice
Vegetable oil spray	1 teaspoon chili powder
2 tablespoons butter	Chopped fresh green onion (optional)
60 g sour cream	
60 g mayonnaise	Chopped fresh coriander (optional)
20 g grated Parmesan cheese (or feta, cotija, or queso fresco)	

Place the corn in the bottom of the air fryer basket and spray with vegetable oil spray. Set the air fryer to 180°C for 10 minutes.

Transfer the corn to a serving bowl. Add the butter and stir until melted. Add the sour cream, mayonnaise, cheese, lemon juice, and chili powder; stir until well combined. Serve immediately with green onion and coriander (if using).

Roasted Potatoes and Asparagus

Prep time: 5 minutes | Cook time: 23 minutes | Serves 4

4 medium potatoes	1 tablespoon wholegrain mustard
1 bunch asparagus	
75 g cottage cheese	Salt and pepper, to taste
80 g low-fat crème fraiche	Cooking spray

Preheat the air fryer to 200°C. Spritz the air fryer basket with cooking spray.

Place the potatoes in the basket. Air fry the potatoes for 20 minutes. Boil the asparagus in salted water for 3 minutes.

Remove the potatoes and mash them with rest of ingredients. Sprinkle with salt and pepper.

Serve immediately.

Tingly Chili-Roasted Broccoli

Prep time: 5 minutes | Cook time: 10 minutes | Serves 2

340 g broccoli florets	1 (2-inch) piece fresh ginger, peeled and finely chopped
2 tablespoons Asian hot chili oil	
1 teaspoon ground Sichuan peppercorns (or black pepper)	coarse sea salt and freshly ground black pepper, to taste
2 garlic cloves, finely chopped	

In a bowl, toss together the broccoli, chili oil, Sichuan peppercorns, garlic, ginger, and salt and black pepper to taste.

Transfer to the air fryer and roast at 192°C, shaking the basket halfway through, until lightly charred and tender, about 10 minutes. Remove from the air fryer and serve warm.

Cauliflower Steaks Gratin

Prep time: 10 minutes | Cook time: 13 minutes | Serves 2

1 head cauliflower	thyme leaves
1 tablespoon olive oil	3 tablespoons grated Parmigiano-Reggiano cheese
Salt and freshly ground black pepper, to taste	
½ teaspoon chopped fresh	2 tablespoons panko bread crumbs

Preheat the air fryer to 192°C.

Cut two steaks out of the centre of the cauliflower. To do this, cut the cauliflower in half and then cut one slice about 1-inch thick off each half. The rest of the cauliflower will fall apart into florets, which you can roast on their own or save for another meal.

Brush both sides of the cauliflower steaks with olive oil and season with salt, freshly ground black pepper and fresh thyme. Place the cauliflower steaks into the air fryer basket and air fry for 6 minutes. Turn the steaks over and air fry for another 4 minutes. Combine the Parmesan cheese and panko bread crumbs and sprinkle the mixture over the tops of both steaks and air fry for another 3 minutes until the cheese has melted and the bread crumbs have browned. Serve this with some sautéed bitter greens and air-fried blistered tomatoes.

Sweet-and-Sour Brussels Sprouts

Prep time: 10 minutes | Cook time: 20 minutes | Serves 2

70 g Thai sweet chili sauce

2 tablespoons black vinegar or balsamic vinegar

½ teaspoon hot sauce, such as Tabasco

230 g Brussels sprouts, trimmed (large sprouts halved)

2 small shallots, cut into ¼-inch-thick slices

coarse sea salt and freshly ground black pepper, to taste

2 teaspoons lightly packed fresh coriander leaves

In a large bowl, whisk together the chili sauce, vinegar, and hot sauce. Add the Brussels sprouts and shallots, season with salt and pepper, and toss to combine. Scrape the Brussels sprouts and sauce into a cake pan.

Place the pan in the air fryer and roast at 192ºC, stirring every 5 minutes, until the Brussels sprouts are tender and the sauce is reduced to a sticky glaze, about 20 minutes.

Remove the pan from the air fryer and transfer the Brussels sprouts to plates. Sprinkle with the coriander and serve warm.

Fried Courgette Salad

Prep time: 10 minutes | Cook time: 5 to 7 minutes | Serves 4

2 medium courgette, thinly sliced

5 tablespoons olive oil, divided

15 g chopped fresh parsley

2 tablespoons chopped fresh mint

Zest and juice of ½ lemon

1 clove garlic, minced

65 g crumbled feta cheese

Freshly ground black pepper, to taste

Preheat the air fryer to 200ºC.

In a large bowl, toss the courgette slices with 1 tablespoon of the olive oil.

Working in batches if necessary, arrange the courgette slices in an even layer in the air fryer basket. Pausing halfway through the cooking time to shake the basket, air fry for 5 to 7 minutes until soft and lightly browned on each side.

Meanwhile, in a small bowl, combine the remaining 4 tablespoons olive oil, parsley, mint, lemon zest, lemon juice, and garlic.

Arrange the courgette on a plate and drizzle with the dressing. Sprinkle the feta and black pepper on top. Serve warm or at room temperature.

Rosemary-Roasted Red Potatoes

Prep time: 5 minutes | Cook time: 20 minutes | Serves 6

450 g red potatoes, quartered

65 ml olive oil

½ teaspoon coarse sea salt

¼ teaspoon black pepper

1 garlic clove, minced

4 rosemary sprigs

Preheat the air fryer to 180ºC.

In a large bowl, toss the potatoes with the olive oil, salt, pepper, and garlic until well coated.

Pour the potatoes into the air fryer basket and top with the sprigs of rosemary.

Roast for 10 minutes, then stir or toss the potatoes and roast for 10 minutes more.

Remove the rosemary sprigs and serve the potatoes. Season with additional salt and pepper, if needed.

Curry Roasted Cauliflower

Prep time: 10 minutes | Cook time: 20 minutes | Serves 4

65 ml olive oil

2 teaspoons curry powder

½ teaspoon salt

¼ teaspoon freshly ground black pepper

1 head cauliflower, cut into bite-size florets

½ red onion, sliced

2 tablespoons freshly chopped parsley, for garnish (optional)

Preheat the air fryer to 200ºC.

In a large bowl, combine the olive oil, curry powder, salt, and pepper. Add the cauliflower and onion. Toss gently until the vegetables are completely coated with the oil mixture. Transfer the vegetables to the basket of the air fryer.

Pausing about halfway through the cooking time to shake the basket, air fry for 20 minutes until the cauliflower is tender and beginning to brown. Top with the parsley, if desired, before serving.

Lush Vegetable Salad

Prep time: 15 minutes | Cook time: 10 minutes | Serves 4

6 plum tomatoes, halved

2 large red onions, sliced

4 long red pepper, sliced

2 yellow pepper, sliced

6 cloves garlic, crushed

1 tablespoon extra-virgin olive oil

1 teaspoon paprika

½ lemon, juiced

Salt and ground black pepper, to taste

1 tablespoon baby capers

Preheat the air fryer to 220°C.

Put the tomatoes, onions, peppers, and garlic in a large bowl and cover with the extra-virgin olive oil, paprika, and lemon juice. Sprinkle with salt and pepper as desired.

Line the inside of the air fryer basket with aluminum foil. Put the vegetables inside and air fry for 10 minutes, ensuring the edges turn brown.

Serve in a salad bowl with the baby capers.

Asparagus Fries

Prep time: 15 minutes | Cook time: 5 to 7 minutes per batch | Serves 4

340 g fresh asparagus spears with tough ends trimmed off

2 egg whites

60 ml water

80 g panko bread crumbs

25 g grated Parmesan cheese, plus 2 tablespoons

¼ teaspoon salt

Oil for misting or cooking spray

Preheat the air fryer to 200°C.

In a shallow dish, beat egg whites and water until slightly foamy.

In another shallow dish, combine panko, Parmesan, and salt.

Dip asparagus spears in egg, then roll in crumbs. Spray with oil or cooking spray.

Place a layer of asparagus in air fryer basket, leaving just a little space in between each spear. Stack another layer on top, crosswise. Air fry at 200°C for 5 to 7 minutes, until crispy and golden brown.

Repeat to cook remaining asparagus.

Chapter 5 Poultry

Chapter 5 Poultry

Blackened Cajun Chicken Tenders

Prep time: 10 minutes | Cook time: 17 minutes | Serves 4

2 teaspoons paprika

1 teaspoon chili powder

½ teaspoon garlic powder

½ teaspoon dried thyme

¼ teaspoon onion powder

⅛ teaspoon ground cayenne

pepper

2 tablespoons coconut oil

450 g boneless, skinless chicken tenders

60 ml full-fat ranch dressing

In a small bowl, combine all seasonings.

Drizzle oil over chicken tenders and then generously coat each tender in the spice mixture. Place tenders into the air fryer basket. Adjust the temperature to (190ºC and air fry for 17 minutes. Tenders will be 76ºC internally when fully cooked. Serve with ranch dressing for dipping.

Pork Rind Fried Chicken

Prep time: 30 minutes | Cook time: 20 minutes | Serves 4

60 ml buffalo sauce

4 (115 g) boneless, skinless chicken breasts

½ teaspoon paprika

½ teaspoon garlic powder

¼ teaspoon ground black pepper

60 g g plain pork rinds, finely crushed

Pour buffalo sauce into a large sealable bowl or bag. Add chicken and toss to coat. Place sealed bowl or bag into refrigerator and let marinate at least 30 minutes up to overnight.

Remove chicken from marinade but do not shake excess sauce off chicken. Sprinkle both sides of thighs with paprika, garlic powder, and pepper.

Place pork rinds into a large bowl and press each chicken breast into pork rinds to coat evenly on both sides.

Place chicken into ungreased air fryer basket. Adjust the temperature to 200ºC and roast for 20 minutes, turning chicken halfway through cooking. Chicken will be golden and have an internal temperature of at least 76ºC when done. Serve warm.

Thai Tacos with Peanut Sauce

Prep time: 10 minutes | Cook time: 6 minutes | Serves 4

450 g chicken mince

10 g diced onions (about 1 small onion)

2 cloves garlic, minced

¼ teaspoon fine sea salt

Sauce:

60 g creamy peanut butter, room temperature

2 tablespoons chicken broth, plus more if needed

2 tablespoons lime juice

2 tablespoons grated fresh ginger

2 tablespoons wheat-free tamari or coconut aminos

1½ teaspoons hot sauce

5 drops liquid stevia (optional)

For Serving:

2 small heads butter lettuce, leaves separated

Lime slices (optional)

For Garnish (Optional):

Coriander leaves

Shredded purple cabbage

Sliced green onions

Preheat the air fryer to 180ºC. .

Place the chicken mince, onions, garlic, and salt in a pie pan or a dish that will fit in your air fryer. Break up the chicken with a spatula. Place in the air fryer and bake for 5 minutes, or until the chicken is browned and cooked through. Break up the chicken again into small crumbles.

Make the sauce: In a medium-sized bowl, stir together the peanut butter, broth, lime juice, ginger, tamari, hot sauce, and stevia (if using) until well combined. If the sauce is too thick, add another tablespoon or two of broth. Taste and add more hot sauce if desired. Add half of the sauce to the pan with the chicken. Cook for another minute, until heated through, and stir well to combine.

Assemble the tacos: Place several lettuce leaves on a serving plate. Place a few tablespoons of the chicken mixture in each lettuce leaf and garnish with coriander leaves, purple cabbage, and sliced green onions, if desired. Serve the remaining sauce on the side. Serve with lime slices, if desired.

Store leftover meat mixture in an airtight container in the refrigerator for up to 4 days; store leftover sauce, lettuce leaves, and garnishes separately. Reheat the meat mixture in a lightly greased pie pan in a preheated 180ºC air fryer for 3 minutes, or until heated through.

Chicken Schnitzel

Prep time: 15 minutes | Cook time: 5 minutes | Serves 4

60 g all-purpose flour

1 teaspoon marjoram

½ teaspoon thyme

1 teaspoon dried parsley flakes

½ teaspoon salt

1 egg

1 teaspoon lemon juice

1 teaspoon water

120 g breadcrumbs

4 chicken tenders, pounded thin, cut in half lengthwise

Cooking spray

Preheat the air fryer to 200ºC and spritz with cooking spray.

Combine the flour, marjoram, thyme, parsley, and salt in a shallow dish. Stir to mix well.

Whisk the egg with lemon juice and water in a large bowl. Pour the breadcrumbs in a separate shallow dish.

Roll the chicken halves in the flour mixture first, then in the egg mixture, and then roll over the breadcrumbs to coat well. Shake the excess off.

Arrange the chicken halves in the preheated air fryer and spritz with cooking spray on both sides.

Air fry for 5 minutes or until the chicken halves are golden brown and crispy. Flip the halves halfway through.

Serve immediately.

Chicken Thighs in Waffles

Prep time: 1 hour 20 minutes | Cook time: 40 minutes | Serves 4

For the chicken:

4 chicken thighs, skin on

240 ml low-fat buttermilk

65 g all-purpose flour

½ teaspoon garlic powder

½ teaspoon mustard powder

1 teaspoon kosher salt

½ teaspoon freshly ground black pepper

85 g honey, for serving

Cooking spray

For the waffles:

65 g all-purpose flour

65 g whole wheat pastry flour

1 large egg, beaten

240 ml low-fat buttermilk

1 teaspoon baking powder

2 tablespoons rapeseed oil

½ teaspoon kosher salt

1 tablespoon granulated sugar

Combine the chicken thighs with buttermilk in a large bowl. Wrap the bowl in plastic and refrigerate to marinate for at least an hour.

Preheat the air fryer to 180ºC. Spritz the air fryer basket with cooking spray.

Combine the flour, mustard powder, garlic powder, salt, and black pepper in a shallow dish. Stir to mix well.

Remove the thighs from the buttermilk and pat dry with paper towels. Sit the bowl of buttermilk aside.

Dip the thighs in the flour mixture first, then into the buttermilk, and then into the flour mixture. Shake the excess off.

Arrange 2 thighs in the preheated air fryer and spritz with cooking spray. Air fryer for 20 minutes or until an instant-read thermometer inserted in the thickest part of the chicken thighs registers at least 76ºC. Flip the thighs halfway through. Repeat with remaining thighs.

Meanwhile, make the waffles: combine the ingredients for the waffles in a large bowl. Stir to mix well, then arrange the mixture in a waffle iron and cook until a golden and fragrant waffle forms.

Remove the waffles from the waffle iron and slice into 4 pieces. Remove the chicken thighs from the air fryer and allow to cool for 5 minutes.

Arrange each chicken thigh on each waffle piece and drizzle with 1 tablespoon of honey. Serve warm.

Yakitori

Prep time: 10 minutes | Cook time: 15 minutes | Serves 4

120 ml mirin

60 ml dry white wine

120 ml soy sauce

1 tablespoon light brown sugar

680 g boneless, skinless chicken thighs, cut into 1½-inch pieces, fat trimmed

4 medium spring onions,

trimmed, cut into 1½-inch pieces

Cooking spray

Special Equipment:

4 (4-inch) bamboo skewers, soaked in water for at least 30 minutes

Combine the mirin, dry white wine, soy sauce, and brown sugar in a saucepan. Bring to a boil over medium heat. Keep stirring.

Boil for another 2 minutes or until it has a thick consistency. Turn off the heat.

Preheat the air fryer to 200ºC. Spritz the air fryer basket with cooking spray.

Run the bamboo skewers through the chicken pieces and spring onions alternatively.

Arrange the skewers in the preheated air fryer, then brush with mirin mixture on both sides. Spritz with cooking spray.

Air fry for 10 minutes or until the chicken and spring onions are glossy. Flip the skewers halfway through.

Serve immediately.

Coriander Lime Chicken Thighs

Prep time: 15 minutes | Cook time: 22 minutes | Serves 4

4 bone-in, skin-on chicken thighs	2 teaspoons chili powder
1 teaspoon baking powder	1 teaspoon cumin
½ teaspoon garlic powder	2 medium limes
	5 g chopped fresh coriander

Pat chicken thighs dry and sprinkle with baking powder.

In a small bowl, mix garlic powder, chili powder, and cumin and sprinkle evenly over thighs, gently rubbing on and under chicken skin.

Cut one lime in half and squeeze juice over thighs. Place chicken into the air fryer basket.

Adjust the temperature to 190ºC and roast for 22 minutes.

Cut other lime into four wedges for serving and garnish cooked chicken with wedges and coriander.

Chicken with Bacon and Tomato

Prep time: 25 minutes | Cook time: 10 minutes | Serves 4

4 medium-sized skin-on chicken drumsticks	2 tablespoons olive oil
1½ teaspoons herbs de Provence	2 garlic cloves, crushed
Salt and pepper, to taste	340 g crushed canned tomatoes
1 tablespoon rice vinegar	1 small-size leek, thinly sliced
	2 slices smoked bacon, chopped

Sprinkle the chicken drumsticks with herbs de Provence, salt and pepper; then, drizzle them with rice vinegar and olive oil.

Cook in the baking pan at 180ºC for 8 to 10 minutes. Pause the air fryer; stir in the remaining ingredients and continue to cook for 15 minutes longer; make sure to check them periodically. Bon appétit!

Yellow Curry Chicken Thighs with Peanuts

Prep time: 10 minutes | Cook time: 20 minutes | Serves 6

120 ml unsweetened full-fat coconut milk	1 tablespoon minced garlic
2 tablespoons yellow curry paste	1 teaspoon kosher salt
1 tablespoon minced fresh ginger	450 g boneless, skinless chicken thighs, halved crosswise
	2 tablespoons chopped peanuts

In a large bowl, stir together the coconut milk, curry paste, ginger, garlic, and salt until well blended. Add the chicken; toss well to coat. Marinate at room temperature for 30 minutes, or cover and refrigerate for up to 24 hours.

Preheat the air fryer to 190ºC.

Place the chicken (along with marinade) in a baking pan. Place the pan in the air fryer basket. Bake for 20 minutes, turning the chicken halfway through the cooking time. Use a meat thermometer to ensure the chicken has reached an internal temperature of 76ºC.

Sprinkle the chicken with the chopped peanuts and serve.

Piri-Piri Chicken Thighs

Prep time: 5 minutes | Cook time: 25 minutes | Serves 4

60 ml piri-piri sauce	1 tablespoon extra-virgin olive oil
1 tablespoon freshly squeezed lemon juice	4 bone-in, skin-on chicken thighs, each weighing approximately 200 to 230 g
2 tablespoons brown sugar, divided	½ teaspoon cornflour
2 cloves garlic, minced	

To make the marinade, whisk together the piri-piri sauce, lemon juice, 1 tablespoon of brown sugar, and the garlic in a small bowl. While whisking, slowly pour in the oil in a steady stream and continue to whisk until emulsified. Using a skewer, poke holes in the chicken thighs and place them in a small glass dish. Pour the marinade over the chicken and turn the thighs to coat them with the sauce. Cover the dish and refrigerate for at least 15 minutes and up to 1 hour.

Preheat the air fryer to 190ºC. Remove the chicken thighs from the dish, reserving the marinade, and place them skin-side down in the air fryer basket. Air fry until the internal temperature reaches 76ºC, 15 to 20 minutes.

Meanwhile, whisk the remaining brown sugar and the cornflour into the marinade and microwave it on high power for 1 minute until it is bubbling and thickened to a glaze.

Once the chicken is cooked, turn the thighs over and brush them with the glaze. Air fry for a few additional minutes until the glaze browns and begins to char in spots.

Remove the chicken to a platter and serve with additional piri-piri sauce, if desired.

Cajun-Breaded Chicken Bites

Prep time: 10 minutes | Cook time: 12 minutes | Serves 4

450 g boneless, skinless chicken breasts, cut into 1-inch cubes	30 g plain pork rinds, finely crushed
120 g heavy whipping cream	40 g unflavoured whey protein powder
½ teaspoon salt	
¼ teaspoon ground black pepper	½ teaspoon Cajun seasoning

Place chicken in a medium bowl and pour in cream. Stir to coat. Sprinkle with salt and pepper.

In a separate large bowl, combine pork rinds, protein powder, and Cajun seasoning. Remove chicken from cream, shaking off any excess, and toss in dry mix until fully coated.

Place bites into ungreased air fryer basket. Adjust the temperature to 200ºC and air fry for 12 minutes, shaking the basket twice during cooking. Bites will be done when golden brown and have an internal temperature of at least 76ºC. Serve warm.

Spicy Chicken Thighs and Gold Potatoes

Prep time: 5 minutes | Cook time: 25 minutes | Serves 4

4 bone-in, skin-on chicken thighs	½ teaspoon dry mustard
½ teaspoon kosher salt or ¼ teaspoon fine salt	½ teaspoon granulated garlic
2 tablespoons melted unsalted butter	¼ teaspoon paprika
	¼ teaspoon hot pepper sauce
2 teaspoons Worcestershire sauce	Cooking oil spray
2 teaspoons curry powder	4 medium Yukon gold potatoes, chopped
1 teaspoon dried oregano leaves	1 tablespoon extra-virgin olive oil

Sprinkle the chicken thighs on both sides with salt.

In a medium bowl, stir together the melted butter, Worcestershire sauce, curry powder, oregano, dry mustard, granulated garlic, paprika, and hot pepper sauce. Add the thighs to the sauce and stir to coat.

Insert the crisper plate into the basket and the basket into the unit. Preheat the unit by selecting AIR FRY, setting the temperature to 200ºC, and setting the time to 3 minutes. Select START/STOP to begin.

Once the unit is preheated, spray the crisper plate with cooking oil.

In the basket, combine the potatoes and olive oil and toss to coat. Add the wire rack to the air fryer and place the chicken thighs on top.

Select AIR FRY, set the temperature to 200ºC, and set the time to 25 minutes. Select START/STOP to begin.

After 19 minutes check the chicken thighs. If a food thermometer inserted into the chicken registers 76ºC, transfer them to a clean plate, and cover with aluminum foil to keep warm. If they aren't cooked to 76ºC, resume cooking for another 1 to 2 minutes until they are done. Remove them from the unit along with the rack.

Remove the basket and shake it to distribute the potatoes. Reinsert the basket to resume cooking for 3 to 6 minutes, or until the potatoes are crisp and golden brown.

When the cooking is complete, serve the chicken with the potatoes.

Golden Tenders

Prep time: 10 minutes | Cook time: 15 minutes | Serves 4

120 g panko bread crumbs	pepper
1 tablespoon paprika	16 chicken tenders
½ teaspoon salt	115 g mayonnaise
¼ teaspoon freshly ground black	Olive oil spray

In a medium bowl, stir together the panko, paprika, salt, and pepper. In a large bowl, toss together the chicken tenders and mayonnaise to coat. Transfer the coated chicken pieces to the bowl of seasoned panko and dredge to coat thoroughly. Press the coating onto the chicken with your fingers.

Insert the crisper plate into the basket and the basket into the unit. Preheat the unit by selecting AIR FRY, setting the temperature to 180ºC, and setting the time to 3 minutes. Select START/STOP to begin.

Once the unit is preheated, place a parchment paper liner into the basket. Place the chicken into the basket and spray it with olive oil. Select AIR FRY, set the temperature to 180ºC, and set the time to 15 minutes. Select START/STOP to begin.

When the cooking is complete, the tenders will be golden brown and a food thermometer inserted into the chicken should register 76ºC. For more even browning, remove the basket halfway through cooking and flip the tenders. Give them an extra spray of olive oil and reinsert the basket to resume cooking. This ensures they are crispy and brown all over.

When the cooking is complete, serve.

Garlic Dill Wings

Prep time: 5 minutes | Cook time: 25 minutes | Serves 4

900 g bone-in chicken wings, separated at joints

½ teaspoon salt

½ teaspoon ground black pepper

½ teaspoon onion powder

½ teaspoon garlic powder

1 teaspoon dried dill

In a large bowl, toss wings with salt, pepper, onion powder, garlic powder, and dill until evenly coated. Place wings into ungreased air fryer basket in a single layer, working in batches if needed.

Adjust the temperature to 200°C and air fry for 25 minutes, shaking the basket every 7 minutes during cooking. Wings should have an internal temperature of at least 76°C and be golden brown when done. Serve warm.

Chicken Hand Pies

Prep time: 30 minutes | Cook time: 10 minutes per batch | Makes 8 pies

180 ml chicken broth

130 g frozen mixed peas and carrots

140 g cooked chicken, chopped

1 tablespoon cornflour

1 tablespoon milk

Salt and pepper, to taste

1 (8-count) can organic flaky biscuits

Oil for misting or cooking spray

In a medium saucepan, bring chicken broth to a boil. Stir in the frozen peas and carrots and cook for 5 minutes over medium heat. Stir in chicken.

Mix the cornflour into the milk until it dissolves. Stir it into the simmering chicken broth mixture and cook just until thickened.

Remove from heat, add salt and pepper to taste, and let cool slightly.

Lay biscuits out on wax paper. Peel each biscuit apart in the middle to make 2 rounds so you have 16 rounds total. Using your hands or a rolling pin, flatten each biscuit round slightly to make it larger and thinner.

Divide chicken filling among 8 of the biscuit rounds. Place remaining biscuit rounds on top and press edges all around. Use the tines of a fork to crimp biscuit edges and make sure they are sealed well.

Spray both sides lightly with oil or cooking spray.

Cook in a single layer, 4 at a time, at 170°C for 10 minutes or until biscuit dough is cooked through and golden brown.

Peachy Chicken Chunks with Cherries

Prep time: 8 minutes | Cook time: 14 to 16 minutes | Serves 4

100 g peach preserves

1 teaspoon ground rosemary

½ teaspoon black pepper

½ teaspoon salt

½ teaspoon marjoram

1 teaspoon light olive oil

450 g boneless chicken breasts, cut in 1½-inch chunks

Oil for misting or cooking spray

1 (280 g) package frozen unsweetened dark cherries, thawed and drained

In a medium bowl, mix together peach preserves, rosemary, pepper, salt, marjoram, and olive oil.

Stir in chicken chunks and toss to coat well with the preserve mixture.

Spray the air fryer basket with oil or cooking spray and lay chicken chunks in basket.

Air fry at 200°C for 7 minutes. Stir. Cook for 6 to 8 more minutes or until chicken juices run clear.

When chicken has cooked through, scatter the cherries over and cook for additional minute to heat cherries.

Lemon Chicken with Garlic

Prep time: 5 minutes | Cook time: 20 to 25 minutes | Serves 4

8 bone-in chicken thighs, skin on

1 tablespoon olive oil

1½ teaspoons lemon-pepper seasoning

½ teaspoon paprika

½ teaspoon garlic powder

¼ teaspoon freshly ground black pepper

Juice of ½ lemon

Preheat the air fryer to 180°C.

Place the chicken in a large bowl and drizzle with the olive oil. Top with the lemon-pepper seasoning, paprika, garlic powder, and freshly ground black pepper. Toss until thoroughly coated.

Working in batches if necessary, arrange the chicken in a single layer in the basket of the air fryer. Pausing halfway through the cooking time to turn the chicken, air fry for 20 to 25 minutes, until a thermometer inserted into the thickest piece registers 76°C.

Transfer the chicken to a serving platter and squeeze the lemon juice over the top.

Butter and Bacon Chicken

Prep time: 10 minutes | Cook time: 65 minutes | Serves 6

1 (1.8 kg) whole chicken

2 tablespoons salted butter, softened

1 teaspoon dried thyme

½ teaspoon garlic powder

1 teaspoon salt

½ teaspoon ground black pepper

6 slices sugar-free bacon

Pat chicken dry with a paper towel, then rub with butter on all sides. Sprinkle thyme, garlic powder, salt, and pepper over chicken. Place chicken into ungreased air fryer basket, breast side up. Lay strips of bacon over chicken and secure with toothpicks.

Adjust the temperature to 180ºC and air fry for 65 minutes. Halfway through cooking, remove and set aside bacon and flip chicken over. Chicken will be done when the skin is golden and crispy and the internal temperature is at least 76ºC. Serve warm with bacon.

Broccoli Cheese Chicken

Prep time: 15 minutes | Cook time: 25 minutes | Serves 4

1 tablespoon avocado oil

15 g chopped onion

35 g finely chopped broccoli

115 g cream cheese, at room temperature

60 g Cheddar cheese, shredded

1 teaspoon garlic powder

½ teaspoon sea salt, plus

additional for seasoning, divided

¼ freshly ground black pepper, plus additional for seasoning, divided

900 g boneless, skinless chicken breasts

1 teaspoon smoked paprika

Heat a medium skillet over medium-high heat and pour in the avocado oil. Add the onion and broccoli and cook, stirring occasionally, for 5 to 8 minutes, until the onion is tender.

Transfer to a large bowl and stir in the cream cheese, Cheddar cheese, and garlic powder, and season to taste with salt and pepper. Hold a sharp knife parallel to the chicken breast and cut a long pocket into one side. Stuff the chicken pockets with the broccoli mixture, using toothpicks to secure the pockets around the filling. In a small dish, combine the paprika, ½ teaspoon salt, and ¼ teaspoon pepper. Sprinkle this over the outside of the chicken.

Set the air fryer to 200ºC. Place the chicken in a single layer in the air fryer basket, cooking in batches if necessary, and cook for 14 to 16 minutes, until an instant-read thermometer reads 70ºC. Place the chicken on a plate and tent a piece of aluminum foil over the chicken. Allow to rest for 5 to 10 minutes before serving.

Gold Livers

Prep time: 10 minutes | Cook time: 20 minutes | Serves 4

2 eggs

2 tablespoons water

90 g flour

240 g panko breadcrumbs

1 teaspoon salt

½ teaspoon ground black pepper

570 g chicken livers

Cooking spray

Preheat the air fryer to 200ºC. Spritz the air fryer basket with cooking spray.

Whisk the eggs with water in a large bowl. Pour the flour in a separate bowl. Pour the panko on a shallow dish and sprinkle with salt and pepper.

Dredge the chicken livers in the flour. Shake the excess off, then dunk the livers in the whisked eggs, and then roll the livers over the panko to coat well.

Arrange the livers in the preheated air fryer and spritz with cooking spray. Work in batches to avoid overcrowding.

Air fry for 10 minutes or until the livers are golden and crispy. Flip the livers halfway through. Repeat with remaining livers.

Serve immediately.

Apricot-Glazed Turkey Tenderloin

Prep time: 20 minutes | Cook time: 30 minutes | Serves 4

Olive oil

80 g sugar-free apricot preserves

½ tablespoon spicy brown mustard

680 g turkey breast tenderloin

Salt and freshly ground black pepper, to taste

Spray the air fryer basket lightly with olive oil.

In a small bowl, combine the apricot preserves and mustard to make a paste.

Season the turkey with salt and pepper. Spread the apricot paste all over the turkey.

Place the turkey in the air fryer basket and lightly spray with olive oil.

Air fry at 190ºC for 15 minutes. Flip the turkey over and lightly spray with olive oil. Air fry until the internal temperature reaches at least 80ºC, an additional 10 to 15 minutes.

Let the turkey rest for 10 minutes before slicing and serving.

Chipotle Aioli Wings

Prep time: 5 minutes | Cook time: 25 minutes | Serves 6

900 g bone-in chicken wings	2 tablespoons mayonnaise
½ teaspoon salt	2 teaspoons chipotle powder
¼ teaspoon ground black pepper	2 tablespoons lemon juice

In a large bowl, toss wings in salt and pepper, then place into ungreased air fryer basket. Adjust the temperature to 200ºC and air fry for 25 minutes, shaking the basket twice while cooking. Wings will be done when golden and have an internal temperature of at least 76ºC.

In a small bowl, whisk together mayonnaise, chipotle powder, and lemon juice. Place cooked wings into a large serving bowl and drizzle with aioli. Toss to coat. Serve warm.

Buttermilk Breaded Chicken

Prep time: 7 minutes | Cook time: 20 to 25 minutes | Serves 4

125 g all-purpose flour	2 tablespoons extra-virgin olive oil
2 teaspoons paprika	
Pinch salt	185 g bread crumbs
Freshly ground black pepper, to taste	6 chicken pieces, drumsticks, breasts, and thighs, patted dry
80 ml buttermilk	Cooking oil spray
2 eggs	

In a shallow bowl, stir together the flour, paprika, salt, and pepper.

In another bowl, beat the buttermilk and eggs until smooth.

In a third bowl, stir together the olive oil and bread crumbs until mixed.

Dredge the chicken in the flour, dip in the eggs to coat, and finally press into the bread crumbs, patting the crumbs firmly onto the chicken skin.

Insert the crisper plate into the basket and the basket into the unit. Preheat the unit by selecting AIR FRY, setting the temperature to 190ºC, and setting the time to 3 minutes. Select START/STOP to begin.

Once the unit is preheated, spray the crisper plate with cooking oil. Place the chicken into the basket.

Select AIR FRY, set the temperature to 190ºC, and set the time to 25 minutes. Select START/STOP to begin.

After 10 minutes, flip the chicken. Resume cooking. After 10 minutes more, check the chicken. If a food thermometer inserted into the chicken registers 76ºC and the chicken is brown and crisp, it is done. Otherwise, resume cooking for up to 5 minutes longer. When the cooking is complete, let cool for 5 minutes, then serve.

Sriracha-Honey Chicken Nuggets

Prep time: 15 minutes | Cook time: 19 minutes | Serves 6

Oil, for spraying	½ teaspoon freshly ground black pepper
1 large egg	
180 ml milk	2 boneless, skinless chicken breasts, cut into bite-size pieces
125 g all-purpose flour	
2 tablespoons icing sugar	140 g barbecue sauce
½ teaspoon paprika	2 tablespoons honey
½ teaspoon salt	1 tablespoon Sriracha

Line the air fryer basket with parchment and spray lightly with oil.

In a small bowl, whisk together the egg and milk.

In a medium bowl, combine the flour, icing sugar, paprika, salt, and black pepper and stir.

Coat the chicken in the egg mixture, then dredge in the flour mixture until evenly coated.

Place the chicken in the prepared basket and spray liberally with oil.

Air fry at 200ºC for 8 minutes, flip, spray with more oil, and cook for another 6 to 8 minutes, or until the internal temperature reaches 76ºC and the juices run clear.

In a large bowl, mix together the barbecue sauce, honey, and Sriracha.

Transfer the chicken to the bowl and toss until well coated with the barbecue sauce mixture.

Line the air fryer basket with fresh parchment, return the chicken to the basket, and cook for another 2 to 3 minutes, until browned and crispy.

Tex-Mex Chicken Breasts

Prep time: 10 minutes | Cook time: 17 to 20 minutes | Serves 4

450 g low-sodium boneless, skinless chicken breasts, cut into 1-inch cubes

1 medium onion, chopped

1 red bell pepper, chopped

1 jalapeño pepper, minced

2 teaspoons olive oil

115 g canned low-sodium black beans, rinsed and drained

130 g low-sodium salsa

2 teaspoons chili powder

Preheat the air fryer to 200°C.

In a medium metal bowl, mix the chicken, onion, bell pepper, jalapeño, and olive oil. Roast for 10 minutes, stirring once during cooking. Add the black beans, salsa, and chili powder. Roast for 7 to 10 minutes more, stirring once, until the chicken reaches an internal temperature of 76°C on a meat thermometer. Serve immediately.

Chapter 6 Fish and Seafood

Chapter 6 Fish and Seafood

Firecracker Prawns

Prep time: 10 minutes | Cook time: 7 minutes | Serves 4

455 g medium prawns, peeled and deveined

2 tablespoons salted butter, melted

½ teaspoon Old Bay seasoning

¼ teaspoon garlic powder

2 tablespoons Sriracha

¼ teaspoon powdered sweetener

60 ml full-fat mayonnaise

⅛ teaspoon ground black pepper

In a large bowl, toss prawns in butter, Old Bay seasoning, and garlic powder. Place prawns into the air fryer basket.

Adjust the temperature to 204ºC and set the timer for 7 minutes.

Flip the prawns halfway through the cooking time. Prawns will be bright pink when fully cooked.

In another large bowl, mix Sriracha, sweetener, mayonnaise, and pepper. Toss prawns in the spicy mixture and serve immediately.

Snapper with Fruit

Prep time: 15 minutes | Cook time: 9 to 13 minutes | Serves 4

4 red snapper fillets, 100 g each

2 teaspoons olive oil

3 nectarines, halved and pitted

3 plums, halved and pitted

150 g red grapes

1 tablespoon freshly squeezed lemon juice

1 tablespoon honey

½ teaspoon dried thyme

Put the red snapper in the air fryer basket and drizzle with the olive oil. Air fry at 200ºC for 4 minutes.

Remove the basket and add the nectarines and plums. Scatter the grapes over all.

Drizzle with the lemon juice and honey and sprinkle with the thyme.

Return the basket to the air fryer and air fry for 5 to 9 minutes more, or until the fish flakes when tested with a fork and the fruit is tender. Serve immediately.

Crab Cakes with Bell Peppers

Prep time: 5 minutes | Cook time: 10 minutes | Serves 4

230 g jumbo lump crab meat

1 egg, beaten

Juice of ½ lemon

50 g bread crumbs

35 g diced green bell pepper

35 g diced red bell pepper

60 g mayonnaise

1 tablespoon Old Bay seasoning

1 teaspoon plain flour

Cooking spray

Preheat the air fryer to 190ºC.

Make the crab cakes: Place all the ingredients except the flour and oil in a large bowl and stir until well incorporated.

Divide the crab mixture into four equal portions and shape each portion into a patty with your hands. Top each patty with a sprinkle of ¼ teaspoon of flour.

Arrange the crab cakes in the air fryer basket and spritz them with cooking spray.

Air fry for 10 minutes, flipping the crab cakes halfway through, or until they are cooked through.

Divide the crab cakes among four plates and serve.

Lemon-Pepper Trout

Prep time: 5 minutes | Cook time: 15 minutes | Serves 4

4 trout fillets

2 tablespoons olive oil

½ teaspoon salt

1 teaspoon black pepper

2 garlic cloves, sliced

1 lemon, sliced, plus additional wedges for serving

Preheat the air fryer to 192ºC.

Brush each fillet with olive oil on both sides and season with salt and pepper. Place the fillets in an even layer in the air fryer basket.

Place the sliced garlic over the tops of the trout fillets, then top the garlic with lemon slices and roast for 12 to 15 minutes, or until it has reached an internal temperature of 64ºC.

Serve with fresh lemon wedges.

Bacon-Wrapped Scallops

Prep time: 5 minutes | Cook time: 10 minutes | Serves 4

8 sea scallops, 30 g each, cleaned and patted dry

8 slices bacon

¼ teaspoon salt

¼ teaspoon ground black pepper

Wrap each scallop in 1 slice bacon and secure with a toothpick. Sprinkle with salt and pepper.

Place scallops into ungreased air fryer basket. Adjust the temperature to 182°C and air fry for 10 minutes. Scallops will be opaque and firm, and have an internal temperature of 56°C when done. Serve warm.

Jalea

Prep time: 20 minutes | Cook time: 10 minutes | Serves 4

Salsa Criolla:

½ red onion, thinly sliced

2 tomatoes, diced

1 serrano or jalapeño pepper, deseeded and diced

1 clove garlic, minced

5 g chopped fresh coriander

Pinch of kosher or coarse sea salt

3 limes

Fried Seafood:

455 g firm, white-fleshed fish such as cod (add an extra 230 g fish if not using prawns)

20 large or jumbo prawns, peeled and deveined

30 g plain flour

40 g cornflour

1 teaspoon garlic powder

1 teaspoon kosher or coarse sea salt

¼ teaspoon cayenne pepper

240 g panko bread crumbs

2 eggs, beaten with 2 tablespoons water

Vegetable oil, for spraying

Mayonnaise or tartar sauce, for serving (optional)

To make the Salsa Criolla, combine the red onion, tomatoes, pepper, garlic, cilantro, and salt in a medium bowl. Add the juice and zest of 2 of the limes. Refrigerate the salad while you make the fish.

To make the seafood, cut the fish fillets into strips approximately 2 inches long and 1 inch wide. Place the flour, cornstarch, garlic powder, salt, and cayenne pepper on a plate and whisk to combine. Place the panko on a separate plate. Dredge the fish strips in the seasoned flour mixture, shaking off any excess. Dip the strips in the egg mixture, coating them completely, then dredge in the panko, shaking off any excess. Place the fish strips on a plate or rack. Repeat with the prawns, if using.

Spray the air fryer basket with oil, and preheat the air fryer to 204°C. Working in 2 or 3 batches, arrange the fish and prawns in a single layer in the basket, taking care not to crowd the basket. Spray with oil. Air fry for 5 minutes, then flip and air fry for another 4 to 5 minutes until the outside is brown and crisp and the inside of the fish is opaque and flakes easily with a fork. Repeat with the remaining seafood.

Place the fried seafood on a platter. Use a slotted spoon to remove the salsa criolla from the bowl, leaving behind any liquid that has accumulated. Place the salsa criolla on top of the fried seafood. Serve immediately with the remaining lime, cut into wedges, and mayonnaise or tartar sauce as desired.

Pesto Fish Pie

Prep time: 15 minutes | Cook time: 15 minutes | Serves 4

2 tablespoons prepared pesto

60 ml single cream

20 g grated Parmesan cheese

1 teaspoon kosher or coarse sea salt

1 teaspoon black pepper

Vegetable oil spray

280 g frozen chopped spinach,

thawed and squeezed dry

455 g firm white fish, cut into 2-inch chunks

115 g cherry tomatoes, quartered

Plain flour

½ sheet frozen puff pastry (from a 490 g package), thawed

In a small bowl, combine the pesto, single cream, Parmesan, salt, and pepper. Stir until well combined; set aside.

Spray a baking pan with vegetable oil spray. Arrange the spinach evenly across the bottom of the pan. Top with the fish and tomatoes. Pour the pesto mixture evenly over everything.

On a lightly floured surface, roll the puff pastry sheet into a circle. Place the pastry on top of the pan and tuck it in around the edges of the pan. (Or, do what I do and stretch it with your hands and then pat it into place.)

Place the pan in the air fryer basket. Set the air fryer to 204°C for 15 minutes, or until the pastry is well browned. Let stand 5 minutes before serving.

Snapper with Shallot and Tomato

Prep time: 20 minutes | Cook time: 15 minutes | Serves 2

2 snapper fillets

1 shallot, peeled and sliced

2 garlic cloves, halved

1 bell pepper, sliced

1 small-sized serrano pepper, sliced

1 tomato, sliced

1 tablespoon olive oil

¼ teaspoon freshly ground black pepper

½ teaspoon paprika

Sea salt, to taste

2 bay leaves

Place two baking paper sheets on a working surface. Place the fish in the center of one side of the baking paper.

Top with the shallot, garlic, peppers, and tomato. Drizzle olive oil over the fish and vegetables. Season with black pepper, paprika, and salt. Add the bay leaves.

Fold over the other half of the baking paper. Now, fold the paper around the edges tightly and create a half moon shape, sealing the fish inside.

Cook in the preheated air fryer at 200°C for 15 minutes. Serve warm.

Prawn Caesar Salad

Prep time: 30 minutes | Cook time: 4 to 6 minutes | Serves 4

340 g fresh large prawns, peeled and deveined

1 tablespoon plus 1 teaspoon freshly squeezed lemon juice, divided

4 tablespoons olive oil or avocado oil, divided

2 garlic cloves, minced, divided

¼ teaspoon sea salt, plus additional to season the marinade

¼ teaspoon freshly ground black pepper, plus additional to season the marinade

735 g mayonnaise

2 tablespoons freshly grated Parmesan cheese

1 teaspoon Dijon mustard

1 tinned anchovy, mashed

340 g romaine lettuce hearts, torn

Place the prawns in a large bowl. Add 1 tablespoon of lemon juice, 1 tablespoon of olive oil, and 1 minced garlic clove. Season with salt and pepper. Toss well and refrigerate for 15 minutes.

While the prawns marinates, make the dressing: In a blender, combine the mayonnaise, Parmesan cheese, Dijon mustard, the remaining 1 teaspoon of lemon juice, the anchovy, the remaining minced garlic clove, ¼ teaspoon of salt, and ¼ teaspoon of pepper. Process until smooth. With the blender running, slowly stream in the remaining 3 tablespoons of oil. Transfer the mixture to a jar; seal and refrigerate until ready to serve.

Remove the prawns from its marinade and place it in the air fryer basket in a single layer. Set the air fryer to 204°C and air fry for 2 minutes. Flip the prawns and cook for 2 to 4 minutes more, until the flesh turns opaque.

Place the romaine in a large bowl and toss with the desired amount of dressing. Top with the prawns and serve immediately.

Baked Grouper with Tomatoes and Garlic

Prep time: 5 minutes | Cook time: 12 minutes | Serves 4

4 grouper fillets

½ teaspoon salt

3 garlic cloves, minced

1 tomato, sliced

45 g sliced Kalamata olives

10 g fresh dill, roughly chopped

Juice of 1 lemon

¼ cup olive oil

Preheat the air fryer to 192°C.

Season the grouper fillets on all sides with salt, then place into the air fryer basket and top with the minced garlic, tomato slices, olives, and fresh dill.

Drizzle the lemon juice and olive oil over the top of the grouper, then bake for 10 to 12 minutes, or until the internal temperature reaches 64°C.

Baked Salmon with Tomatoes and Olives

Prep time: 5 minutes | Cook time: 8 minutes | Serves 4

2 tablespoons olive oil

4 (1½-inch-thick) salmon fillets

½ teaspoon salt

¼ teaspoon cayenne

1 teaspoon chopped fresh dill

2 plum tomatoes, diced

45 g sliced Kalamata olives

4 lemon slices

Preheat the air fryer to 192°C.

Brush the olive oil on both sides of the salmon fillets, and then season them lightly with salt, cayenne, and dill.

Place the fillets in a single layer in the basket of the air fryer, then layer the tomatoes and olives over the top. Top each fillet with a lemon slice.

Bake for 8 minutes, or until the salmon has reached an internal temperature of 64°C.

Crab Cake Sandwich

Prep time: 15 minutes | Cook time: 10 minutes | Serves 4

Crab Cakes:

60 g panko bread crumbs

1 large egg, beaten

1 large egg white

1 tablespoon mayonnaise

1 teaspoon Dijon mustard

5 g minced fresh parsley

1 tablespoon fresh lemon juice

½ teaspoon Old Bay seasoning

⅛ teaspoon sweet paprika

⅛ teaspoon kosher or coarse sea salt

Freshly ground black pepper, to

taste

280 g lump crab meat

Cooking spray

Cajun Mayo:

60 g mayonnaise

1 tablespoon minced dill pickle

1 teaspoon fresh lemon juice

¾ teaspoon Cajun seasoning

For Serving:

4 round lettuce leaves

4 whole wheat potato buns or gluten-free buns

For the crab cakes: In a large bowl, combine the panko, whole egg, egg white, mayonnaise, mustard, parsley, lemon juice, Old Bay, paprika, salt, and pepper to taste and mix well. Fold in the crab meat, being careful not to over mix. Gently shape into 4 round patties, ¾ inch thick. Spray both sides with oil.

Preheat the air fryer to 188°C.

Working in batches, place the crab cakes in the air fryer basket. Air fry for about 10 minutes, flipping halfway, until the edges are golden.

Meanwhile, for the Cajun mayo: In a small bowl, combine the mayonnaise, pickle, lemon juice, and Cajun seasoning.

To serve: Place a lettuce leaf on each bun bottom and top with a crab cake and a generous tablespoon of Cajun mayonnaise. Add the bun top and serve.

Garlicky Cod Fillets

Prep time: 10 minutes | Cook time: 10 to 12 minutes | Serves 4

1 teaspoon olive oil

4 cod fillets

¼ teaspoon fine sea salt

¼ teaspoon ground black pepper, or more to taste

1 teaspoon cayenne pepper

8 g fresh Italian parsley,

coarsely chopped

120 ml milk

1 Italian pepper, chopped

4 garlic cloves, minced

1 teaspoon dried basil

½ teaspoon dried oregano

Lightly coat the sides and bottom of a baking dish with the olive oil. Set aside.

In a large bowl, sprinkle the fillets with salt, black pepper, and cayenne pepper.

In a food processor, pulse the remaining ingredients until smoothly puréed.

Add the purée to the bowl of fillets and toss to coat, then transfer to the prepared baking dish.

Preheat the air fryer to 192°C.

Put the baking dish in the air fryer basket and bake for 10 to 12 minutes, or until the fish flakes when pressed lightly with a fork. Remove from the basket and serve warm.

Air Fried Spring Rolls

Prep time: 10 minutes | Cook time: 17 to 22 minutes | Serves 4

2 teaspoons minced garlic

180 g finely sliced cabbage

50 g matchstick cut carrots

2 cans tiny prawns, 110 g each, drained

4 teaspoons soy sauce

Salt and freshly ground black pepper, to taste

16 square spring roll wrappers

Cooking spray

Preheat the air fryer to 188°C.

Spray the air fryer basket lightly with cooking spray. Spray a medium sauté pan with cooking spray.

Add the garlic to the sauté pan and cook over medium heat until fragrant, 30 to 45 seconds. Add the cabbage and carrots and sauté until the vegetables are slightly tender, about 5 minutes.

Add the prawns and soy sauce and season with salt and pepper, then stir to combine. Sauté until the moisture has evaporated, 2 more minutes. Set aside to cool.

Place a spring roll wrapper on a work surface so it looks like a diamond. Place 1 tablespoon of the prawn mixture on the lower end of the wrapper.

Roll the wrapper away from you halfway, then fold in the right and left sides, like an envelope. Continue to roll to the very end, using a little water to seal the edge. Repeat with the remaining wrappers and filling.

Place the spring rolls in the air fryer basket in a single layer, leaving room between each roll. Lightly spray with cooking spray. You may need to cook them in batches.

Air fry for 5 minutes. Turn the rolls over, lightly spray with cooking spray, and air fry until heated through and the rolls start to brown, 5 to 10 more minutes. Cool for 5 minutes before serving.

Cornmeal-Crusted Trout Fingers

Prep time: 15 minutes | Cook time: 6 minutes | Serves 2

70 g yellow cornmeal, medium or finely ground (not coarse)

40 g plain flour

1½ teaspoons baking powder

1 teaspoon kosher or coarse sea salt, plus more as needed

½ teaspoon freshly ground black pepper, plus more as needed

⅛ teaspoon cayenne pepper

340 g skinless trout fillets, cut

into strips 1 inch wide and 3 inches long

3 large eggs, lightly beaten

Cooking spray

115 g mayonnaise

2 tablespoons capers, rinsed and finely chopped

1 tablespoon fresh tarragon

1 teaspoon fresh lemon juice, plus lemon wedges, for serving

Preheat the air fryer to 204ºC.

In a large bowl, whisk together the cornmeal, flour, baking powder, salt, black pepper, and cayenne. Dip the trout strips in the egg, then toss them in the cornmeal mixture until fully coated. Transfer the trout to a rack set over a baking sheet and liberally spray all over with cooking spray.

Transfer half the fish to the air fryer and air fry until the fish is cooked through and golden brown, about 6 minutes. Transfer the fish sticks to a plate and repeat with the remaining fish.

Meanwhile, in a bowl, whisk together the mayonnaise, capers, tarragon, and lemon juice. Season the tartar sauce with salt and black pepper.

Serve the trout fingers hot along with the tartar sauce and lemon wedges.

Snapper Scampi

Prep time: 5 minutes | Cook time: 8 to 10 minutes | Serves 4

4 skinless snapper or arctic char fillets, 170 g each

1 tablespoon olive oil

3 tablespoons lemon juice, divided

½ teaspoon dried basil

Pinch salt

Freshly ground black pepper, to taste

2 tablespoons butter

2 cloves garlic, minced

Rub the fish fillets with olive oil and 1 tablespoon of the lemon juice. Sprinkle with the basil, salt, and pepper, and place in the air fryer basket.

Air fry the fish at 192ºC for 7 to 8 minutes or until the fish just flakes when tested with a fork. Remove the fish from the basket and put on a serving plate. Cover to keep warm.

In a baking pan, combine the butter, remaining 2 tablespoons lemon juice, and garlic. Bake in the air fryer for 1 to 2 minutes or until the garlic is sizzling. Pour this mixture over the fish and serve

Fish Taco Bowl

Prep time: 10 minutes | Cook time: 12 minutes | Serves 4

½ teaspoon salt

¼ teaspoon garlic powder

¼ teaspoon ground cumin

4 cod fillets, 110 g each

360 g finely shredded green

cabbage

735 g mayonnaise

¼ teaspoon ground black pepper

20 g chopped pickled jalapeños

Sprinkle salt, garlic powder, and cumin over cod and place into ungreased air fryer basket. Adjust the temperature to 176ºC and air fry for 12 minutes, turning fillets halfway through cooking. Cod will flake easily and have an internal temperature of at least 64ºC when done.

In a large bowl, toss cabbage with mayonnaise, pepper, and jalapeños until fully coated. Serve cod warm over cabbage slaw on four medium plates.

Southern-Style Catfish

Prep time: 10 minutes | Cook time: 12 minutes | Serves 4

4 (200 g) catfish fillets

80 ml heavy whipping cream

1 tablespoon lemon juice

110 g blanched finely ground

almond flour

2 teaspoons Old Bay seasoning

½ teaspoon salt

¼ teaspoon ground black pepper

Place catfish fillets into a large bowl with cream and pour in lemon juice. Stir to coat.

In a separate large bowl, mix flour and Old Bay seasoning.

Remove each fillet and gently shake off excess cream. Sprinkle with salt and pepper. Press each fillet gently into flour mixture on both sides to coat.

Place fillets into ungreased air fryer basket. Adjust the temperature to 204ºC and air fry for 12 minutes, turning fillets halfway through cooking. Catfish will be golden brown and have an internal temperature of at least 64ºC when done. Serve warm.

Confetti Salmon Burgers

Prep time: 10 minutes | Cook time: 12 minutes | Serves 4

400 g cooked fresh or canned salmon, flaked with a fork

40 g minced spring onions, white and light green parts only

40 g minced red bell pepper

40 g minced celery

2 small lemons

1 teaspoon crab boil seasoning such as Old Bay

½ teaspoon kosher or coarse sea salt

½ teaspoon black pepper

1 egg, beaten

30 g fresh bread crumbs

Vegetable oil, for spraying

In a large bowl, combine the salmon, vegetables, the zest and juice of 1 of the lemons, crab boil seasoning, salt, and pepper. Add the egg and bread crumbs and stir to combine. Form the mixture into 4 patties weighing approximately 140 g each. Chill until firm, about 15 minutes.

Preheat the air fryer to 204°C.

Spray the salmon patties with oil on all sides and spray the air fryer basket to prevent sticking. Air fry for 12 minutes, flipping halfway through, until the burgers are browned and cooked through. Cut the remaining lemon into 4 wedges and serve with the burgers.

Salmon Spring Rolls

Prep time: 20 minutes | Cook time: 8 to 10 minutes | Serves 4

230 g salmon fillet

1 teaspoon toasted sesame oil

1 onion, sliced

8 rice paper wrappers

1 yellow bell pepper, thinly sliced

1 carrot, shredded

10 g chopped fresh flat-leaf parsley

15 g chopped fresh basil

Put the salmon in the air fryer basket and drizzle with the sesame oil. Add the onion. Air fry at 188°C for 8 to 10 minutes, or until the salmon just flakes when tested with a fork and the onion is tender.

Meanwhile, fill a small shallow bowl with warm water. One at a time, dip the rice paper wrappers into the water and place on a work surface.

Top each wrapper with one-eighth each of the salmon and onion mixture, yellow bell pepper, carrot, parsley, and basil. Roll up the wrapper, folding in the sides, to enclose the ingredients.

If you like, bake in the air fryer at 192°C for 7 to 9 minutes, until the rolls are crunchy. Cut the rolls in half to serve.

Chapter 7 Beef, Pork, and Lamb

Chapter 7 Beef, Pork, and Lamb

Simple Beef Mince with Courgette

Prep time: 5 minutes | Cook time: 12 minutes | Serves 4

680 g beef mince	1 teaspoon dried basil
450 g chopped courgette	1 teaspoon dried rosemary
2 tablespoons extra-virgin olive oil	2 tablespoons fresh chives, chopped
1 teaspoon dried oregano	

Preheat the air fryer to 204°C.

In a large bowl, combine all the ingredients, except for the chives, until well blended.

Place the beef and courgette mixture in the baking pan. Air fry for 12 minutes, or until the beef is browned and the courgette is tender. Divide the beef and courgette mixture among four serving dishes. Top with fresh chives and serve hot.

Sausage-Stuffed Peppers

Prep time: 15 minutes | Cook time: 28 to 30 minutes | Serves 6

Avocado oil spray	black pepper, to taste
230 g Italian-seasoned sausage, casings removed	235 ml keto-friendly marinara sauce
120 ml chopped mushrooms	3 peppers, halved and seeded
60 ml diced onion	85 g low-moisture Mozzarella or other melting cheese, shredded
1 teaspoon Italian seasoning	
Sea salt and freshly ground	

Spray a large skillet with oil and place it over medium-high heat. Add the sausage and cook for 5 minutes, breaking up the meat with a wooden spoon. Add the mushrooms, onion, and Italian seasoning, and season with salt and pepper. Cook for 5 minutes more. Stir in the marinara sauce and cook until heated through.

Scoop the sausage filling into the pepper halves.

Set the air fryer to 176°C. Arrange the peppers in a single layer in the air fryer basket, working in batches if necessary. Air fry for 15 minutes.

Top the stuffed peppers with the cheese and air fry for 3 to 5 minutes more, until the cheese is melted and the peppers are tender.

Easy Beef Satay

Prep time: 30 minutes | Cook time: 8 minutes | Serves 4

450 g beef bavette or skirt steak, thinly sliced into long strips	1 tablespoon minced garlic
	1 tablespoon sugar
2 tablespoons vegetable oil	1 teaspoon Sriracha or other hot sauce
1 tablespoon fish sauce	
1 tablespoon soy sauce	1 teaspoon ground coriander
1 tablespoon minced fresh ginger	120 ml chopped fresh coriander
	60 ml chopped roasted peanuts

Place the beef strips in a large bowl or resealable plastic bag. Add the vegetable oil, fish sauce, soy sauce, ginger, garlic, sugar, Sriracha, coriander, and 60 ml of the fresh coriander to the bag. Seal and massage the bag to thoroughly coat and combine. Marinate at room temperature for 30 minutes, or cover and refrigerate for up to 24 hours.

Using tongs, remove the beef strips from the bag and lay them flat in the air fryer basket, minimizing overlap as much as possible; discard the marinade. Set the air fryer to 204°C for 8 minutes, turning the beef strips halfway through the cooking time.

Transfer the meat to a serving platter. Sprinkle with the remaining 60 ml coriander and the peanuts. Serve.

Garlic Balsamic London Broil

Prep time: 30 minutes | Cook time: 8 to 10 minutes | Serves 8

900 g bavette or skirt steak	2 tablespoons olive oil
3 large garlic cloves, minced	Sea salt and ground black pepper, to taste
3 tablespoons balsamic vinegar	
3 tablespoons wholegrain mustard	½ teaspoon dried hot red pepper flakes

Score both sides of the cleaned steak.

Thoroughly combine the remaining ingredients; massage this mixture into the meat to coat it on all sides. Let it marinate for at least 3 hours.

Set the air fryer to 204°C; Then cook the steak for 15 minutes. Flip it over and cook another 10 to 12 minutes. Bon appétit!

Bone-in Pork Chops

Prep time: 5 minutes | Cook time: 10 to 12 minutes | Serves 2

450 g bone-in pork chops

1 tablespoon avocado oil

1 teaspoon smoked paprika

½ teaspoon onion granules

¼ teaspoon cayenne pepper

Sea salt and freshly ground black pepper, to taste

Brush the pork chops with the avocado oil. In a small dish, mix together the smoked paprika, onion granules, cayenne pepper, and salt and black pepper to taste. Sprinkle the seasonings over both sides of the pork chops.

Set the air fryer to 204ºC. Place the chops in the air fryer basket in a single layer, working in batches if necessary. Air fry for 10 to 12 minutes, until an instant-read thermometer reads 64ºC at the chops' thickest point.

Remove the chops from the air fryer and allow them to rest for 5 minutes before serving.

Filipino Crispy Pork Belly

Prep time: 20 minutes | Cook time: 30 minutes | Serves 4

450 g pork belly

700 ml water

6 garlic cloves

2 tablespoons soy sauce

1 teaspoon coarse or flaky salt

1 teaspoon black pepper

2 bay leaves

Cut the pork belly into three thick chunks so it will cook more evenly.

Place the pork, water, garlic, soy sauce, salt, pepper, and bay leaves in the inner pot of an Instant Pot or other electric pressure cooker. Seal and cook at high pressure for 15 minutes. Let the pressure release naturally for 10 minutes, then manually release the remaining pressure. (If you do not have a pressure cooker, place all the ingredients in a large saucepan. Cover and cook over low heat until a knife can be easily inserted into the skin side of pork belly, about 1 hour.) Using tongs, very carefully transfer the meat to a wire rack over a rimmed baking sheet to drain and dry for 10 minutes.

Cut each chunk of pork belly into two long slices. Arrange the slices in the air fryer basket. Set the air fryer to 204ºC for 15 minutes, or until the fat has crisped.

Serve immediately.

Savory Sausage Cobbler

Prep time: 15 minutes | Cook time: 34 minutes | Serves 4

Filling:

450 g Italian-seasoned sausage meat, removed from casing

235 ml sliced mushrooms

1 teaspoon fine sea salt

475 ml marinara sauce

Biscuits:

3 large egg whites

180 ml blanched almond flour

1 teaspoon baking powder

¼ teaspoon fine sea salt

2½ tablespoons very cold unsalted butter, cut into ¼-inch pieces

Fresh basil leaves, for garnish

Preheat the air fryer to 204ºC.

Place the sausage in a pie pan (or a pan that fits into your air fryer). Use your hands to break up the sausage and spread it evenly on the bottom of the pan. Place the pan in the air fryer and air fry for 5 minutes.

Remove the pan from the air fryer and use a fork or metal spatula to crumble the sausage more. Season the mushrooms with the salt and add them to the pie pan. Stir to combine the mushrooms and sausage, then return the pan to the air fryer and air fry for 4 minutes, or until the mushrooms are soft and the sausage is cooked through.

Remove the pan from the air fryer. Add the marinara sauce and stir well. Set aside.

Make the biscuits: Place the egg whites in a large mixing bowl or the bowl of a stand mixer. Using a hand mixer or stand mixer, whip the egg whites until stiff peaks form.

In a medium-sized bowl, whisk together the almond flour, baking powder, and salt, then cut in the butter. Gently fold the flour mixture into the egg whites with a rubber spatula.

Using a large spoon or ice cream scoop, spoon one-quarter of the dough on top of the sausage mixture, making sure the butter stays in separate clumps. Repeat with the remaining dough, spacing the biscuits about 1 inch apart.

Place the pan in the air fryer and cook for 5 minutes, then lower the heat to 164ºC and bake for another 15 to 20 minutes, until the biscuits are golden brown. Serve garnished with fresh basil leaves.

Store leftovers in an airtight container in the refrigerator for up to 3 days. Reheat in a preheated 176ºC air fryer for 5 minutes, or until warmed through.

Panko Crusted Calf's Liver Strips

Prep time: 15 minutes | Cook time: 23 to 25 minutes | Serves 4

450 g sliced calf's liver, cut into ½-inch wide strips

2 eggs

2 tablespoons milk

120 ml whole wheat flour

475 ml panko breadcrumbs

Salt and ground black pepper, to taste

Cooking spray

Preheat the air fryer to 200ºC and spritz with cooking spray.

Rub the calf's liver strips with salt and ground black pepper on a clean work surface.

Whisk the eggs with milk in a large bowl. Pour the flour in a shallow dish. Pour the panko on a separate shallow dish.

Dunk the liver strips in the flour, then in the egg mixture. Shake the excess off and roll the strips over the panko to coat well.

Arrange half of the liver strips in a single layer in the preheated air fryer and spritz with cooking spray.

Air fry for 5 minutes or until browned. Flip the strips halfway through. Repeat with the remaining strips.

Serve immediately.

Steaks with Walnut-Blue Cheese Butter

Prep time: 30 minutes | Cook time: 10 minutes | Serves 6

120 ml unsalted butter, at room temperature

120 ml crumbled blue cheese

2 tablespoons finely chopped walnuts

1 tablespoon minced fresh rosemary

1 teaspoon minced garlic

¼ teaspoon cayenne pepper

Sea salt and freshly ground black pepper, to taste

680 g sirloin steaks, at room temperature

In a medium bowl, combine the butter, blue cheese, walnuts, rosemary, garlic, and cayenne pepper and salt and black pepper to taste. Use clean hands to ensure that everything is well combined.

Place the mixture on a sheet of parchment paper and form it into a log. Wrap it tightly in plastic wrap. Refrigerate for at least 2 hours or freeze for 30 minutes.

Season the steaks generously with salt and pepper.

Place the air fryer basket or grill pan in the air fryer. Set the air fryer to 204ºC and let it preheat for 5 minutes.

Place the steaks in the basket in a single layer and air fry for 5 minutes. Flip the steaks, and cook for 5 minutes more, until an instant-read thermometer reads 49ºC for medium-rare (or as desired).

Transfer the steaks to a plate. Cut the butter into pieces and place the desired amount on top of the steaks. Tent a piece of aluminum foil over the steaks and allow to sit for 10 minutes before serving.

Store any remaining butter in a sealed container in the refrigerator for up to 2 weeks.

Blue Cheese Steak Salad

Prep time: 30 minutes | Cook time: 22 minutes | Serves 4

2 tablespoons balsamic vinegar

2 tablespoons red wine vinegar

1 tablespoon Dijon mustard

1 tablespoon granulated sweetener

1 teaspoon minced garlic

Sea salt and freshly ground black pepper, to taste

180 ml extra-virgin olive oil

450 g boneless rump steak

Avocado oil spray

1 small red onion, cut into ¼-inch-thick rounds

170 g baby spinach

120 ml cherry tomatoes, halved

85 g blue cheese, crumbled

In a blender, combine the balsamic vinegar, red wine vinegar, Dijon mustard, sweetener, and garlic. Season with salt and pepper and process until smooth. With the blender running, drizzle in the olive oil. Process until well combined. Transfer to a jar with a tight-fitting lid, and refrigerate until ready to serve (it will keep for up to 2 weeks).

Season the steak with salt and pepper and let sit at room temperature for at least 45 minutes, time permitting.

Set the air fryer to 204ºC. Spray the steak with oil and place it in the air fryer basket. Air fry for 6 minutes. Flip the steak and spray it with more oil. Air fry for 6 minutes more for medium-rare or until the steak is done to your liking.

Transfer the steak to a plate, tent with a piece of aluminum foil, and allow it to rest.

Spray the onion slices with oil and place them in the air fryer basket. Cook at 204ºC for 5 minutes. Flip the onion slices and spray them with more oil. Air fry for 5 minutes more.

Slice the steak diagonally into thin strips. Place the spinach, cherry tomatoes, onion slices, and steak in a large bowl. Toss with the desired amount of dressing. Sprinkle with crumbled blue cheese and serve.

Beefy Poppers

Prep time: 15 minutes | Cook time: 15 minutes | Makes 8 poppers

8 medium jalapeño peppers, stemmed, halved, and seeded

1 (230 g) package cream cheese (or cream cheese style spread for dairy-free), softened

900 g beef mince (85% lean)

1 teaspoon fine sea salt

½ teaspoon ground black pepper

8 slices thin-cut bacon

Fresh coriander leaves, for garnish

Spray the air fryer basket with avocado oil. Preheat the air fryer to 204°C.

Stuff each jalapeño half with a few tablespoons of cream cheese. Place the halves back together again to form 8 jalapeños.

Season the beef mince with the salt and pepper and mix with your hands to incorporate. Flatten about 110 g of beef in the palm of your hand and place a stuffed jalapeño in the center. Fold the beef around the jalapeño, forming an egg shape. Wrap the beef-covered jalapeño with a slice of bacon and secure it with a toothpick.

Place the jalapeños in the air fryer basket, leaving space between them (if you're using a smaller air fryer, work in batches if necessary), and air fry for 15 minutes, or until the beef is cooked through and the bacon is crispy. Garnish with coriander before serving.

Store leftovers in an airtight container in the fridge for 3 days or in the freezer for up to a month. Reheat in a preheated 176°C air fryer for 4 minutes, or until heated through and the bacon is crispy.

Bean and Beef Meatball Taco Pizza

Prep time: 10 minutes | Cook time: 7 to 9 minutes per batch | Serves 4

180 ml refried beans (from a 450 g can)

120 ml salsa

10 frozen precooked beef meatballs, thawed and sliced

1 jalapeño pepper, sliced

4 whole-wheat pitta breads

235 ml shredded chilli cheese

120 ml shredded Monterey Jack or Cheddar cheese

Cooking oil spray

80 ml sour cream

In a medium bowl, stir together the refried beans, salsa, meatballs, and jalapeño.

Insert the crisper plate into the basket and the basket into the unit. Preheat the unit by selecting BAKE, setting the temperature to 192°C, and setting the time to 3 minutes. Select START/STOP to begin.

Top the pittas with the refried bean mixture and sprinkle with the cheeses.

Once the unit is preheated, spray the crisper plate with cooking oil. Working in batches, place the pizzas into the basket. Select BAKE, set the temperature to 192°C, and set the time to 9 minutes. Select START/STOP to begin.

After about 7 minutes, check the pizzas. They are done when the cheese is melted and starts to brown. If not ready, resume cooking. When the cooking is complete, top each pizza with a dollop of sour cream and serve warm.

Greek Stuffed Fillet

Prep time: 10 minutes | Cook time: 10 minutes | Serves 4

680 g venison or beef fillet, pounded to ¼ inch thick

3 teaspoons fine sea salt

1 teaspoon ground black pepper

60 g creamy goat cheese

120 ml crumbled feta cheese (about 60 g)

60 ml finely chopped onions

2 cloves garlic, minced

For Garnish/Serving (Optional):

Yellow/American mustard

Halved cherry tomatoes

Extra-virgin olive oil

Sprigs of fresh rosemary

Lavender flowers

Spray the air fryer basket with avocado oil. Preheat the air fryer to 204°C.

Season the fillet on all sides with the salt and pepper.

In a medium-sized mixing bowl, combine the goat cheese, feta, onions, and garlic. Place the mixture in the center of the tenderloin. Starting at the end closest to you, tightly roll the tenderloin like a jelly roll. Tie the rolled tenderloin tightly with kitchen twine.

Place the meat in the air fryer basket and air fry for 5 minutes. Flip the meat over and cook for another 5 minutes, or until the internal temperature reaches 57°C for medium-rare.

To serve, smear a line of yellow mustard on a platter, then place the meat next to it and add halved cherry tomatoes on the side, if desired. Drizzle with olive oil and garnish with rosemary sprigs and lavender flowers, if desired.

Best served fresh. Store leftovers in an airtight container in the fridge for 3 days. Reheat in a preheated 176°C air fryer for 4 minutes, or until heated through.

Pork and Tricolor Vegetables Kebabs

Prep time: 1 hour 20 minutes | Cook time: 8 minutes per batch | Serves 4

For the Pork:

450 g pork steak, cut in cubes

1 tablespoon white wine vinegar

3 tablespoons steak sauce or brown sauce

60 ml soy sauce

1 teaspoon powdered chili

1 teaspoon red chili flakes

2 teaspoons smoked paprika

1 teaspoon garlic salt

For the Vegetable:

1 courgette, cut in cubes

1 butternut squash, deseeded and cut in cubes

1 red pepper, cut in cubes

1 green pepper, cut in cubes

Salt and ground black pepper, to taste

Cooking spray

Special Equipment:

4 bamboo skewers, soaked in water for at least 30 minutes

Combine the ingredients for the pork in a large bowl. Press the pork to dunk in the marinade. Wrap the bowl in plastic and refrigerate for at least an hour.

Preheat the air fryer to 188ºC and spritz with cooking spray.

Remove the pork from the marinade and run the skewers through the pork and vegetables alternatively. Sprinkle with salt and pepper to taste.

Arrange the skewers in the preheated air fryer and spritz with cooking spray. Air fry for 8 minutes or until the pork is browned and the vegetables are lightly charred and tender. Flip the skewers halfway through. You may need to work in batches to avoid overcrowding.

Serve immediately.

BBQ Pork Steaks

Prep time: 5 minutes | Cook time: 15 minutes | Serves 4

4 pork steaks

1 tablespoon Cajun seasoning

2 tablespoons BBQ sauce

1 tablespoon vinegar

1 teaspoon soy sauce

120 ml brown sugar

120 ml ketchup

1.Preheat the air fryer to 143ºC.

Sprinkle pork steaks with Cajun seasoning.

Combine remaining ingredients and brush onto steaks.

Add coated steaks to air fryer. Air fry 15 minutes until just browned.

Serve immediately.

Bacon Wrapped Pork with Apple Gravy

Prep time: 10 minutes | Cook time: 25 minutes | Serves 4

Pork:

1 tablespoons Dijon mustard

1 pork tenderloin

3 strips bacon

Apple Gravy:

3 tablespoons ghee, divided

1 small shallot, chopped

2 apples

1 tablespoon almond flour

235 ml vegetable stock

½ teaspoon Dijon mustard

Preheat the air fryer to 182ºC.

Spread Dijon mustard all over tenderloin and wrap with strips of bacon.

Put into air fryer and air fry for 12 minutes. Use a meat thermometer to check for doneness.

To make sauce, heat 1 tablespoons of ghee in a pan and add shallots. Cook for 1 minute.

Then add apples, cooking for 4 minutes until softened.

Add flour and 2 tablespoons of ghee to make a roux. Add stock and mustard, stirring well to combine.

When sauce starts to bubble, add 235 ml of sautéed apples, cooking until sauce thickens.

Once pork tenderloin is cooked, allow to sit 8 minutes to rest before slicing.

Serve topped with apple gravy.

Kale and Beef Omelet

Prep time: 15 minutes | Cook time: 16 minutes | Serves 4

230 g leftover beef, coarsely chopped

2 garlic cloves, pressed

235 ml kale, torn into pieces and wilted

1 tomato, chopped

¼ teaspoon sugar

4 eggs, beaten

4 tablespoons double cream

½ teaspoon turmeric powder

Salt and ground black pepper, to taste

⅛ teaspoon ground allspice

Cooking spray

Preheat the air fryer to 182ºC. Spritz four ramekins with cooking spray.

Put equal amounts of each of the ingredients into each ramekin and mix well.

Air fry for 16 minutes. Serve immediately.

Currywurst

Prep time: 15 minutes | Cook time: 12 minutes | Serves 4

235 ml tomato sauce

2 tablespoons cider vinegar

2 teaspoons curry powder

2 teaspoons sweet paprika

1 teaspoon sugar

¼ teaspoon cayenne pepper

1 small onion, diced

450 g bratwurst, sliced diagonally into 1-inch pieces

In a large bowl, combine the tomato sauce, vinegar, curry powder, paprika, sugar, and cayenne. Whisk until well combined. Stir in the onion and bratwurst.

Transfer the mixture to a baking pan. Place the pan in the air fryer basket. Set the air fryer to 204°C for 12 minutes, or until the sausage is heated through and the sauce is bubbling.

Macadamia Nuts Crusted Pork Rack

Prep time: 5 minutes | Cook time: 35 minutes | Serves 2

1 clove garlic, minced

2 tablespoons olive oil

450 g rack of pork

235 ml chopped macadamia nuts

1 tablespoon breadcrumbs

1 tablespoon rosemary, chopped

1 egg

Salt and ground black pepper, to taste

Preheat the air fryer to 176°C.

Combine the garlic and olive oil in a small bowl. Stir to mix well.

On a clean work surface, rub the pork rack with the garlic oil and sprinkle with salt and black pepper on both sides.

Combine the macadamia nuts, breadcrumbs, and rosemary in a shallow dish. Whisk the egg in a large bowl.

Dredge the pork in the egg, then roll the pork over the macadamia nut mixture to coat well. Shake the excess off.

Arrange the pork in the preheated air fryer and air fry for 30 minutes on both sides. Increase to 200°C and fry for 5 more minutes or until the pork is well browned.

Serve immediately.

Marinated Steak Tips with Mushrooms

Prep time: 30 minutes | Cook time: 10 minutes | Serves 4

680 g rump steak, trimmed and cut into 1-inch pieces

230 g brown mushrooms, halved

60 ml Worcestershire sauce

1 tablespoon Dijon mustard

1 tablespoon olive oil

1 teaspoon paprika

1 teaspoon crushed red pepper flakes

2 tablespoons chopped fresh parsley (optional)

Place the beef and mushrooms in a gallon-size resealable bag. In a small bowl, whisk together the Worcestershire, mustard, olive oil, paprika, and red pepper flakes. Pour the marinade into the bag and massage gently to ensure the beef and mushrooms are evenly coated. Seal the bag and refrigerate for at least 4 hours, preferably overnight. Remove from the refrigerator 30 minutes before cooking.

Preheat the air fryer to 204°C.

Drain and discard the marinade. Arrange the steak and mushrooms in the air fryer basket. Air fry for 10 minutes, pausing halfway through the baking time to shake the basket. Transfer to a serving plate and top with the parsley, if desired.

Chapter 8 Pizzas, Wraps, and Sandwiches

Chapter 8 Pizzas, Wraps, and Sandwiches

Pesto Chicken Mini Pizzas

Prep time: 5 minutes | Cook time: 10 minutes | Serves 4

475 ml shredded cooked chicken	4 English muffins, split
180 ml pesto	475 ml shredded Mozzarella cheese

In a medium bowl, toss the chicken with the pesto.

Place one-eighth of the chicken on each English muffin half.

Top each English muffin with 60 ml Mozzarella cheese.

Put four pizzas at a time in the air fryer and air fry at 176°C for 5 minutes.

Repeat this process with the other four pizzas.

Crunchy Chicken and Ranch Wraps

Prep time: 10 minutes | Cook time: 25 minutes | Serves 4

2 (113 g) boneless, skinless breasts	120 ml breadcrumbs
30 ml ranch dressing	Cooking oil
Chicken seasoning or rub	4 medium (8-inch) flour tortillas
235 ml plain flour	350 ml shredded lettuce
1 egg	3 tablespoons ranch dressing

With your knife blade parallel to the cutting board, slice the chicken breasts in half horizontally to create 4 thin cutlets.

Season the chicken cutlets with the ranch dressing and chicken seasoning to taste.

In a bowl large enough to dip a chicken cutlet, beat the egg.

In another bowl, place the flour.

Put the breadcrumbs in a third bowl.

Spray the air fryer basket with cooking oil.

Dip each chicken cutlet in the flour, then the egg, and then the breadcrumbs.

Place the chicken in the air fryer. Do not stack. Cook in batches.

Spray the chicken with cooking oil.

Air fry at 370°F for 7 minutes.

Open the air fryer and flip the chicken.

Cook for an additional 3 to 4 minutes, until crisp.

Remove the cooked chicken from the air fryer and allow to cool for 2 to 3 minutes.

Repeat steps 6 through 8 for the remaining chicken.

Cut the chicken into strips.

Divide the chicken strips, shredded lettuce, and ranch dressing evenly among the tortillas and serve.

Cheesy Veggie Wraps

Prep time: 15 minutes | Cook time: 8 to 10 minutes per batch | Serves 4

227 g green beans	3 tablespoons lemon juice
2 portobello mushroom caps, sliced	¼ teaspoon ground black pepper
1 large red pepper, sliced	4 (6-inch) wholemeal wraps
2 tablespoons olive oil, divided	110 g fresh herb or garlic goat cheese, crumbled
¼ teaspoon salt	1 lemon, cut into wedges
1 (425 g) can chickpeas, drained	

Preheat the air fryer to 204°C.

Add the green beans, mushrooms, red pepper to a large bowl.

Drizzle with 1 tablespoon olive oil and season with salt.

Toss until well coated.

Transfer the vegetable mixture to a baking pan.

Air fry in the preheated air fryer in 2 batches, 8 to 10 minutes per batch, stirring constantly during cooking.

Meanwhile, mash the chickpeas with lemon juice, pepper and the remaining 1 tablespoon oil until well blended Unfold the wraps on a clean work surface.

Spoon the chickpea mash on the wraps and spread all over.

Divide the cooked veggies among wraps.

Sprinkle 30 g crumbled goat cheese on top of each wrap.

Fold to wrap.

Squeeze the lemon wedges on top and serve.

Cheesy Chicken Sandwich

Prep time: 10 minutes | Cook time: 5 to 7 minutes | Serves 1

80 ml chicken, cooked and shredded	1 teaspoon olive oil
2 Mozzarella slices	½ teaspoon balsamic vinegar
1 hamburger bun	¼ teaspoon smoked paprika
60 ml shredded cabbage	¼ teaspoon black pepper
1 teaspoon mayonnaise	¼ teaspoon garlic powder
2 teaspoons butter, melted	Pinch of salt

Preheat the air fryer to 188ºC.

Brush some butter onto the outside of the hamburger bun.

In a bowl, coat the chicken with the garlic powder, salt, pepper, and paprika.

In a separate bowl, stir together the mayonnaise, olive oil, cabbage, and balsamic vinegar to make coleslaw.

Slice the bun in two.

Start building the sandwich, starting with the chicken, followed by the Mozzarella, the coleslaw, and finally the top bun.

Transfer the sandwich to the air fryer and bake for 5 to 7 minutes.

Serve immediately.

Chicken and Pickles Sandwich

Prep time: 30 minutes | Cook time: 25 minutes | Serves 4

2 (113 g) boneless, skinless chicken breasts	1 egg
235 ml dill pickle juice	120 ml plain flour
235 ml milk, divided	Salt and pepper, to taste
Cooking oil	4 buns
	Pickles

With your knife blade parallel to the cutting board, slice the chicken breasts in half horizontally to create 4 thin cutlets.

Place the chicken in a large bowl.

Add the pickle juice and 120 ml of milk and toss to coat.

Allow the chicken to marinate in the refrigerator for at least 30 minutes.

Spray the air fryer basket with cooking oil.

In a bowl large enough to dip a chicken cutlet, beat the egg and add the remaining 120 ml of milk.

Stir to combine.

In another bowl, place the flour and season with salt and pepper.

When done marinating, dip each chicken cutlet in the egg and milk mixture and then the flour.

Place 2 chicken cutlets in the air fryer.

Spray them with cooking oil.

Air fry at 370ºF for 6 minutes.

Open the air fryer and flip the chicken.

Cook for an additional 6 minutes.

Remove the cooked chicken from the air fryer, then repeat steps 7 and 8 for the remaining 2 chicken cutlets.

Serve on buns with pickles.

Mediterranean-Pitta Wraps

Prep time: 5 minutes | Cook time: 14 minutes | Serves 4

450 g mackerel fish fillets	Sea salt and freshly ground black pepper, to taste
2 tablespoons olive oil	
1 tablespoon Mediterranean seasoning mix	60 g feta cheese, crumbled
	4 tortillas
½ teaspoon chilli powder	

Toss the fish fillets with the olive oil; place them in the lightly oiled air fryer basket.

Air fry the fish fillets at 204ºC for about 14 minutes, turning them over halfway through the cooking time.

Assemble your pittas with the chopped fish and remaining ingredients and serve warm.

Mushroom Pitta Pizzas

Prep time: 10 minutes | Cook time: 5 minutes | Serves 4

4 (3-inch) pittas	½ teaspoon dried basil
1 tablespoon olive oil	2 spring onions, minced
180 ml pizza sauce	235 ml grated Mozzarella or provolone cheese
1 (113 g) jar sliced mushrooms, drained	235 ml sliced grape tomatoes

Brush each piece of pitta with oil and top with the pizza sauce.

Add the mushrooms and sprinkle with basil and spring onions.

Top with the grated cheese.

Bake at 182ºC for 3 to 6 minutes or until the cheese is melted and starts to brown.

Top with the grape tomatoes and serve immediately.

Beef and Pepper Fajitas

Prep time: 15 minutes | Cook time: 10 minutes | Serves 4

450 g beef sirloin steak, cut into strips

2 shallots, sliced

1 orange pepper, sliced

1 red pepper, sliced

2 garlic cloves, minced

2 tablespoons Cajun seasoning

1 tablespoon paprika

Salt and ground black pepper, to taste

4 corn tortillas

120 ml shredded Cheddar cheese

Cooking spray

Preheat the air fryer to 182°C and spritz with cooking spray.

Combine all the ingredients, except for the tortillas and cheese, in a large bowl.

Toss to coat well.

Pour the beef and vegetables in the preheated air fryer and spritz with cooking spray.

Air fry for 10 minutes or until the meat is browned and the vegetables are soft and lightly wilted. Shake the basket halfway through.

Unfold the tortillas on a clean work surface and spread the cooked beef and vegetables on top.

Scatter with cheese and fold to serve.

Avocado and Slaw Tacos

Prep time: 15 minutes | Cook time: 6 minutes | Serves 4

60 ml plain flour

¼ teaspoon salt, plus more as needed

¼ teaspoon ground black pepper

2 large egg whites

300 ml panko breadcrumbs

2 tablespoons olive oil

2 avocados, peeled and halved, cut into ½-inch-thick slices

½ small red cabbage, thinly

sliced

1 deseeded jalapeño, thinly sliced

2 spring onions, thinly sliced

120 ml coriander leaves

60 ml mayonnaise

Juice and zest of 1 lime

4 corn tortillas, warmed

120 ml sour cream

Cooking spray

Preheat the air fryer to 204°C.

Spritz the air fryer basket with cooking spray.

Pour the flour in a large bowl and sprinkle with salt and black pepper, then stir to mix well.

Whisk the egg whites in a separate bowl.

Combine the panko with olive oil on a shallow dish.

Dredge the avocado slices in the bowl of flour, then into the egg to coat.

Shake the excess off, then roll the slices over the panko.

Arrange the avocado slices in a single layer in the basket and spritz the cooking spray.

Air fry for 6 minutes or until tender and lightly browned. Flip the slices halfway through with tongs.

Combine the cabbage, jalapeño, onions, coriander leaves, mayo, lime juice and zest, and a touch of salt in a separate large bowl.

Toss to mix well.

Unfold the tortillas on a clean work surface, then spread with cabbage slaw and air fried avocados.

Top with sour cream and serve.

Crispy Chicken Egg Rolls

Prep time: 10 minutes | Cook time: 23 to 24 minutes | Serves 4

450 g minced chicken

2 teaspoons olive oil

2 garlic cloves, minced

1 teaspoon grated fresh ginger

475 ml white cabbage, shredded

1 onion, chopped

60 ml soy sauce

8 egg roll wrappers

1 egg, beaten

Cooking spray

Preheat the air fryer to 188°C.

Spritz the air fryer basket with cooking spray.

Heat olive oil in a saucepan over medium heat.

Sauté the garlic and ginger in the olive oil for 1 minute, or until fragrant.

Add the minced chicken to the saucepan.

Sauté for 5 minutes, or until the chicken is cooked through.

Add the cabbage, onion and soy sauce and sauté for 5 to 6 minutes, or until the vegetables become soft.

Remove the saucepan from the heat.

Unfold the egg roll wrappers on a clean work surface.

Divide the chicken mixture among the wrappers and brush the edges of the wrappers with the beaten egg.

Tightly roll up the egg rolls, enclosing the filling.

Arrange the rolls in the prepared air fryer basket and air fry for 12 minutes, or until crispy and golden brown. Turn halfway through the cooking time to ensure even cooking.

Transfer to a platter and let cool for 5 minutes before serving.

Shrimp and Courgette Curry Potstickers

Prep time: 35 minutes | Cook time: 15 minutes | Serves 10

230 g peeled and deveined shrimp, finely chopped

1 medium courgette, coarsely grated

1 tablespoon fish sauce

1 tablespoon green curry paste

2 spring onions, thinly sliced

60 ml basil, chopped

30 round dumpling wrappers

Cooking spray

Combine the chopped shrimp, courgette, fish sauce, curry paste, spring onions, and basil in a large bowl. Stir to mix well.

Unfold the dumpling wrappers on a clean work surface, dab a little water around the edges of each wrapper, then scoop up 1 teaspoon of filling in the middle of each wrapper.

Make the potstickers: Fold the wrappers in half and press the edges to seal.

Preheat the air fryer to 176°C.

Spritz the air fryer basket with cooking spray.

Transfer 10 potstickers in the basket each time and spritz with cooking spray.

Air fry for 5 minutes or until the potstickers are crunchy and lightly browned. Flip the potstickers halfway through.

Repeat with remaining potstickers.

Serve immediately.

Korean Flavour Beef and Onion Tacos

Prep time: 1 hour 15 minutes | Cook time: 12 minutes | Serves 6

2 tablespoons gochujang chilli sauce

1 tablespoon soy sauce

2 tablespoons sesame seeds

2 teaspoons minced fresh ginger

2 cloves garlic, minced

2 tablespoons toasted sesame oil

2 teaspoons sugar

½ teaspoon rock salt

680 g thinly sliced braising steak

1 medium red onion, sliced

6 corn tortillas, warmed

60 ml chopped fresh coriander

120 ml kimchi

120 ml chopped spring onions

Combine the gochujang, soy sauce, sesame seeds, ginger, garlic, sesame oil, sugar, and salt in a large bowl. Stir to mix well.

Dunk the braising steak in the large bowl.

Press to submerge, then wrap the bowl in plastic and refrigerate to marinate for at least 1 hour.

Preheat the air fryer to 204°C.

Remove the braising steak from the marinade and transfer to the preheated air fryer basket.

Add the onion and air fry for 12 minutes or until well browned.

Shake the basket halfway through.

Unfold the tortillas on a clean work surface, then divide the fried beef and onion on the tortillas.

Spread the coriander, kimchi, and spring onions on top.

Serve immediately.

Barbecue Chicken Pitta Pizza

Prep time: 5 minutes | Cook time: 5 to 7 minutes per batch | Makes 4 pizzas

235 ml barbecue sauce, divided

4 pitta breads

475 ml shredded cooked chicken

475 ml shredded Mozzarella cheese

½ small red onion, thinly sliced

2 tablespoons finely chopped fresh coriander

Measure 120 ml of the barbecue sauce in a small measuring cup.

Spread 2 tablespoons of the barbecue sauce on each pitta.

In a medium bowl, mix together the remaining 120 ml of barbecue sauce and chicken.

Place 120 ml of the chicken on each pitta.

Top each pizza with 120 ml of the Mozzarella cheese.

Sprinkle the tops of the pizzas with the red onion.

Place one pizza in the air fryer.

Air fry at 204°C for 5 to 7 minutes.

Repeat this process with the remaining pizzas.

Top the pizzas with the coriander.

Bacon and Pepper Sandwiches

Prep time: 15 minutes | Cook time: 7 minutes | Serves 4

80 ml spicy barbecue sauce

2 tablespoons honey

8 slices precooked bacon, cut into thirds

1 red pepper, sliced

1 yellow pepper, sliced

3 pitta pockets, cut in half

300 ml torn butterhead lettuce leaves

2 tomatoes, sliced

In a small bowl, combine the barbecue sauce and the honey.

Brush this mixture lightly onto the bacon slices and the red and yellow pepper slices.

Put the peppers into the air fryer basket and air fry at 176°C for 4 minutes.

Then shake the basket, add the bacon, and air fry for 2 minutes or until the bacon is browned and the peppers are tender.

Fill the pitta halves with the bacon, peppers, any remaining barbecue sauce, lettuce, and tomatoes, and serve immediately.

Buffalo Chicken French Bread Pizza

Prep time: 10 minutes | Cook time: 12 minutes | Serves 8

Oil, for spraying

1 loaf French bread, cut in half and split lengthwise

4 tablespoons unsalted butter, melted

475 ml shredded or diced rotisserie chicken

110 g soft white cheese

3 tablespoons buffalo sauce, plus more for serving

2 tablespoons dry ranch seasoning

475 ml shredded Mozzarella cheese

80 ml crumbled blue cheese

Line the air fryer basket with parchment and spray lightly with oil.

Brush the cut sides of the bread with the melted butter.

Place the bread in the prepared basket.

You may need to work in batches, depending on the size of your air fryer.

Air fry at 204°C for 5 to 7 minutes, or until the bread is toasted.

In a medium bowl, mix together the chicken, soft white cheese, buffalo sauce, and ranch seasoning.

Divide the mixture equally among the toasted bread and spread in an even layer.

Top with the Mozzarella cheese and blue cheese and cook for another 3 to 5 minutes, or until the cheese is melted.

Let cool for 2 to 3 minutes before cutting into 2-inch slices.

Serve with additional buffalo sauce for drizzling.

Chapter 9 Vegetarian Mains

Chapter 9 Vegetarian Mains

Crispy Tofu

Prep time: 30 minutes | Cook time: 15 to 20 minutes | Serves 4

1 (454 g) block extra-firm tofu

2 tablespoons coconut aminos

1 tablespoon toasted sesame oil

1 tablespoon olive oil

1 tablespoon chilli-garlic sauce

1½ teaspoons black sesame seeds

1 spring onion, thinly sliced

Press the tofu for at least 15 minutes by wrapping it in paper towels and setting a heavy pan on top so that the moisture drains.

Slice the tofu into bite-size cubes and transfer to a bowl.

Drizzle with the coconut aminos, sesame oil, olive oil, and chilli-garlic sauce.

Cover and refrigerate for 1 hour or up to overnight.

Preheat the air fryer to 204ºC.

Arrange the tofu in a single layer in the air fryer basket.

Pausing to shake the pan halfway through the cooking time, air fry for 15 to 20 minutes until crisp.

Serve with any juices that accumulate in the bottom of the air fryer, sprinkled with the sesame seeds and sliced spring onion.

Crispy Cabbage Steaks

Prep time: 5 minutes | Cook time: 10 minutes | Serves 4

1 small head green cabbage, cored and cut into ½-inch-thick slices

¼ teaspoon salt

¼ teaspoon ground black pepper

2 tablespoons olive oil

1 clove garlic, peeled and finely minced

½ teaspoon dried thyme

½ teaspoon dried parsley

Sprinkle each side of cabbage with salt and pepper, then place into ungreased air fryer basket, working in batches if needed.

Drizzle each side of cabbage with olive oil, then sprinkle with remaining ingredients on both sides.

Adjust the temperature to 176ºC and air fry for 10 minutes, turning "steaks" halfway through cooking. Cabbage will be browned at the edges and tender when done.

Serve warm.

Cheesy Cabbage Wedges

Prep time: 5 minutes | Cook time: 20 minutes | Serves 4

4 tablespoons melted butter

1 head cabbage, cut into wedges

235 ml shredded Parmesan cheese

Salt and black pepper, to taste

120 ml shredded Mozzarella cheese

Preheat the air fryer to 192ºC.

Brush the melted butter over the cut sides of cabbage wedges and sprinkle both sides with the Parmesan cheese.

Season with salt and pepper to taste.

Place the cabbage wedges in the air fryer basket and air fry for 20 minutes, flipping the cabbage halfway through, or until the cabbage wedges are lightly browned.

Transfer the cabbage wedges to a plate and serve with the Mozzarella cheese sprinkled on top.

Whole Roasted Lemon Cauliflower

Prep time: 5 minutes | Cook time: 15 minutes | Serves 4

1 medium head cauliflower

2 tablespoons salted butter, melted

1 medium lemon

½ teaspoon garlic powder

1 teaspoon dried parsley

Remove the leaves from the head of cauliflower and brush it with melted butter.

Cut the lemon in half and zest one half onto the cauliflower.

Squeeze the juice of the zested lemon half and pour it over the cauliflower.

Sprinkle with garlic powder and parsley.

Place cauliflower head into the air fryer basket.

Adjust the temperature to 176ºC and air fry for 15 minutes.

Check cauliflower every 5 minutes to avoid overcooking. It should be fork tender.

To serve, squeeze juice from other lemon half over cauliflower.

Serve immediately.

Lush Summer Rolls

Prep time: 15 minutes | Cook time: 15 minutes | Serves 4

235 ml shiitake mushroom, sliced thinly

1 celery stalk, chopped

1 medium carrot, shredded

½ teaspoon finely chopped ginger

1 teaspoon sugar

1 tablespoon soy sauce

1 teaspoon Engevita yeast flakes

8 spring roll sheets

1 teaspoon corn starch

2 tablespoons water

In a bowl, combine the ginger, soy sauce, Engevita yeast flakes, carrots, celery, mushroom, and sugar.

Mix the cornflour and water to create an adhesive for the spring rolls.

Scoop a tablespoonful of the vegetable mixture into the middle of the spring roll sheets.

Brush the edges of the sheets with the cornflour adhesive and enclose around the filling to make spring rolls.

Preheat the air fryer to 204ºC.

When warm, place the rolls inside and air fry for 15 minutes or until crisp.

Serve hot.

Cayenne Tahini Kale

Prep time: 5 minutes | Cook time: 15 minutes | Serves 2 to 4

Dressing:

60 ml tahini

60 ml fresh lemon juice

2 tablespoons olive oil

1 teaspoon sesame seeds

½ teaspoon garlic powder

¼ teaspoon cayenne pepper

Kale:

1 L packed torn kale leaves (stems and ribs removed and leaves torn into palm-size pieces)

Rock salt and freshly ground black pepper, to taste

Preheat the air fryer to 176ºC.

Make the dressing: Whisk together the tahini, lemon juice, olive oil, sesame seeds, garlic powder, and cayenne pepper in a large bowl until well mixed.

Add the kale and massage the dressing thoroughly all over the leaves.

Sprinkle the salt and pepper to season.

Place the kale in the air fryer basket in a single layer and air fry for about 15 minutes, or until the leaves are slightly wilted and crispy.

Remove from the basket and serve on a plate.

Pesto Spinach Flatbread

Prep time: 10 minutes | Cook time: 8 minutes | Serves 4

235 ml blanched finely ground almond flour

60 g soft white cheese

475 ml shredded Mozzarella

cheese

235 ml chopped fresh spinach leaves

2 tablespoons basil pesto

Place flour, soft white cheese, and Mozzarella in a large microwave-safe bowl and microwave on high 45 seconds, then stir.

Fold in spinach and microwave an additional 15 seconds.

Stir until a soft dough ball forms.

Cut two pieces of parchment paper to fit air fryer basket.

Separate dough into two sections and press each out on ungreased parchment to create 6-inch rounds.

Spread 1 tablespoon pesto over each flatbread and place rounds on parchment into ungreased air fryer basket.

Adjust the temperature to 176ºC and air fry for 8 minutes, turning crusts halfway through cooking. Flatbread will be golden when done.

Let cool 5 minutes before slicing and serving.

Rosemary Beetroots with Balsamic Glaze

Prep time: 5 minutes | Cook time: 10 minutes | Serves 2

Beetroot:

2 beetroots, cubed

2 tablespoons olive oil

2 sprigs rosemary, chopped

Salt and black pepper, to taste

Balsamic Glaze:

80 ml balsamic vinegar

1 tablespoon honey

Preheat the air fryer to 204ºC.

Combine the beetroots, olive oil, rosemary, salt, and pepper in a mixing bowl and toss until the beetroots are completely coated.

Place the beetroots in the air fryer basket and air fry for 10 minutes until the beetroots are crisp and browned at the edges. Shake the basket halfway through the cooking time.

Meanwhile, make the balsamic glaze: Place the balsamic vinegar and honey in a small saucepan and bring to a boil over medium heat.

When the sauce starts to boil, reduce the heat to medium-low heat and simmer until the liquid is reduced by half.

When ready, remove the beetroots from the basket to a platter.

Pour the balsamic glaze over the top and serve immediately.

White Cheddar and Mushroom Soufflés

Prep time: 15 minutes | Cook time: 12 minutes | Serves 4

3 large eggs, whites and yolks separated

120 ml extra mature white Cheddar cheese

85 g soft white cheese

¼ teaspoon cream of tartar

¼ teaspoon salt

¼ teaspoon ground black pepper

120 ml chestnut mushrooms, sliced

In a large bowl, whip egg whites until stiff peaks form, about 2 minutes.

In a separate large bowl, beat Cheddar, egg yolks, soft white cheese, cream of tartar, salt, and pepper together until combined.

Fold egg whites into cheese mixture, being careful not to stir.

Fold in mushrooms, then pour mixture evenly into four ungreased ramekins.

Place ramekins into air fryer basket.

Adjust the temperature to 176ºC and bake for 12 minutes. Eggs will be browned on the top and firm in the centre when done.

Serve warm.

Garlic White Courgette Rolls

Prep time: 20 minutes | Cook time: 20 minutes | Serves 4

2 medium courgette

2 tablespoons unsalted butter

¼ white onion, peeled and diced

½ teaspoon finely minced roasted garlic

60 ml double cream

2 tablespoons vegetable broth

⅛ teaspoon xanthan gum

120 ml full-fat ricotta cheese

¼ teaspoon salt

½ teaspoon garlic powder

¼ teaspoon dried oregano

475 ml spinach, chopped

120 ml sliced baby portobello mushrooms

180 ml shredded Mozzarella cheese, divided

Using a mandoline or sharp knife, slice courgette into long strips lengthwise.

Place strips between paper towels to absorb moisture.

Set aside.

In a medium saucepan over medium heat, melt butter.

Add onion and sauté until fragrant.

Add garlic and sauté 30 seconds.

Pour in double cream, broth, and xanthan gum.

Turn off heat and whisk mixture until it begins to thicken, about 3 minutes.

In a medium bowl, add ricotta, salt, garlic powder, and oregano and mix well.

Fold in spinach, mushrooms, and 120 ml Mozzarella.

Pour half of the sauce into a round baking pan.

To assemble the rolls, place two strips of courgette on a work surface.

Spoon 2 tablespoons of ricotta mixture onto the slices and roll up.

Place seam side down on top of sauce.

Repeat with remaining ingredients.

Pour remaining sauce over the rolls and sprinkle with remaining Mozzarella.

Cover with foil and place into the air fryer basket.

Adjust the temperature to 176ºC and bake for 20 minutes.

In the last 5 minutes, remove the foil to brown the cheese.

Serve immediately.

Fried Root Vegetable Medley with Thyme

Prep time: 10 minutes | Cook time: 22 minutes | Serves 4

2 carrots, sliced

2 potatoes, cut into chunks

1 swede, cut into chunks

1 turnip, cut into chunks

1 beetroot, cut into chunks

8 shallots, halved

2 tablespoons olive oil

Salt and black pepper, to taste

2 tablespoons tomato pesto

2 tablespoons water

2 tablespoons chopped fresh thyme

Preheat the air fryer to 204ºC.

Toss the carrots, potatoes, swede, turnip, beetroot, shallots, olive oil, salt, and pepper in a large mixing bowl until the root vegetables are evenly coated.

Place the root vegetables in the air fryer basket and air fry for 12 minutes.

Shake the basket and air fry for another 10 minutes until they are cooked to your preferred doneness.

Meanwhile, in a small bowl, whisk together the tomato pesto and water until smooth.

When ready, remove the root vegetables from the basket to a platter.

Drizzle with the tomato pesto mixture and sprinkle with the thyme.

Serve immediately.

Quiche-Stuffed Peppers

Prep time: 5 minutes | Cook time: 15 minutes | Serves 2

2 medium green peppers

3 large eggs

60 ml full-fat ricotta cheese

60 ml diced brown onion

120 ml chopped broccoli

120 ml shredded medium Cheddar cheese

Cut the tops off of the peppers and remove the seeds and white membranes with a small knife.

In a medium bowl, whisk eggs and ricotta.

Add onion and broccoli.

Pour the egg and vegetable mixture evenly into each pepper.

Top with Cheddar.

Place peppers into a 1 L round baking dish and place into the air fryer basket.

Adjust the temperature to 176ºC and bake for 15 minutes. Eggs will be mostly firm and peppers tender when fully cooked.

Serve immediately.

Courgette-Ricotta Tart

Prep time: 15 minutes | Cook time: 60 minutes | Serves 6

120 ml grated Parmesan cheese, divided

350 ml almond flour

1 tablespoon coconut flour

½ teaspoon garlic powder

¾ teaspoon salt, divided

60 ml unsalted butter, melted

1 courgette, thinly sliced (about 475 ml)

235 ml ricotta cheese

3 eggs

2 tablespoons double cream

2 cloves garlic, minced

½ teaspoon dried tarragon

Preheat the air fryer to 166ºC.

Coat a round pan with olive oil and set aside.

In a large bowl, whisk 60 ml Parmesan with the almond flour, coconut flour, garlic powder, and ¼ teaspoon of the salt.

Stir in the melted butter until the dough resembles coarse crumbs.

Press the dough firmly into the bottom and up the sides of the prepared pan.

Air fry for 12 to 15 minutes until the crust begins to brown.

Let cool to room temperature.

Meanwhile, place the courgette in a colander and sprinkle with the remaining ½ teaspoon salt.

Toss gently to distribute the salt and let sit for 30 minutes.

Use paper towels to pat the courgette dry.

In a large bowl, whisk together the ricotta, eggs, double cream, garlic, and tarragon.

Gently stir in the courgette slices.

Pour the cheese mixture into the cooled crust and sprinkle with the remaining 60 ml Parmesan.

Increase the air fryer to 176ºC.

Place the pan in the air fryer basket and air fry for 45 to 50 minutes, or until set and a tester inserted into the centre of the tart comes out clean.

Serve warm or at room temperature.

Russet Potato Gratin

Prep time: 10 minutes | Cook time: 35 minutes | Serves 6

120 ml milk

7 medium russet or Maris Piper potatoes, peeled

Salt, to taste

1 teaspoon black pepper

120 ml double cream

120 ml grated semi-mature cheese

½ teaspoon nutmeg

Preheat the air fryer to 200ºC.

Cut the potatoes into wafer-thin slices.

In a bowl, combine the milk and cream and sprinkle with salt, pepper, and nutmeg.

Use the milk mixture to coat the slices of potatoes.

Put in a baking dish.

Top the potatoes with the rest of the milk mixture.

Put the baking dish into the air fryer basket and bake for 25 minutes.

Pour the cheese over the potatoes.

Bake for an additional 10 minutes, ensuring the top is nicely browned before serving.

Potato and Broccoli with Tofu Scramble

Prep time: 15 minutes | Cook time: 30 minutes | Serves 3

600 ml chopped red potato

2 tablespoons olive oil, divided

1 block tofu, chopped finely

2 tablespoons tamari

1 teaspoon turmeric powder

½ teaspoon onion powder

½ teaspoon garlic powder

120 ml chopped onion

1 L broccoli florets

Preheat the air fryer to 204ºC.

Toss together the potatoes and 1 tablespoon of the olive oil.

Air fry the potatoes in a baking dish for 15 minutes, shaking once during the cooking time to ensure they fry evenly.

Combine the tofu, the remaining 1 tablespoon of the olive oil, turmeric, onion powder, tamari, and garlic powder together, stirring in the onions, followed by the broccoli.

Top the potatoes with the tofu mixture and air fry for an additional 15 minutes.

Serve warm.

Printed in Great Britain
by Amazon

13449140R00038